Jesus

The Heart of His Message

Chiara Lubich

Jesus
The Heart of His Message

Unity
and
Jesus Forsaken

New City Press

Published in the United States by New City Press
202 Cardinal Rd., Hyde Park, NY 12538
©1985 New City Press

Translated from the original Italian edition
L'unità e Gesú Abbandonato
©Città Nuova Editrice, Rome, Italy
by Julian Stead, O.S.B.
Introduction translated by M. Angeline Bouchard and Donald Mitchell

Cover design by Nick Cianfarani
Cover painting by Sr. Mary Grace, O.P.

Library of Congress Catalog Number: 85-072397
ISBN 1-56548-090-2

Nihil Obstat: Michael J. Curran, S.T.L., Delegated Censor
Imprimatur: Francis J. Mugavero, D.D., Bishop of Brooklyn
Brooklyn, N.Y., July 29, 1985

1st printing: September 1985
2d printing: January 1997

Printed in the United States of America

Contents

Foreword

*T*o a world marked by complexity and confusion, Chiara Lubich speaks in this book words of Gospel simplicity and clarity.

Even more, to a day when many find in suffering a riddle, she shows how it can lead to happiness, to a deep joy rooted in the Cross of Christ.

Finally, for a human family divided in a thousand ways, she describes the way to unity which is Jesus' gift to us.

This is a book for reading and reflection, a book written in prayer which can nourish prayer. May the Holy Spirit guide each reader to find within its pages fresh help for praying and for living in joy and peace and unity.

William Cardinal Keeler
Archbishop of Baltimore

Introduction

*T*he pages of this book are filled with light. They are given to the world by Chiara Lubich as an urgent message in which are joined two indissoluble realities that call to mind two decisive moments in the life of Jesus: his priestly prayer for unity (Jn 17:21-23), and his cry of abandonment on the cross (Mt 27:46). These two essential realities are unity and Jesus forsaken.

In a letter written in 1948, Chiara Lubich expressed her experience of these two inseparable elements of Christian spirituality: "The book of light that the Lord is writing within my soul has two aspects — a page shining with mysterious love: Unity. A page luminous with mysterious suffering: Jesus forsaken. They are two sides of a single coin."

Chiara Lubich and her Focolare Movement have been living by these two pages of light for more than forty years now. And their worldwide working for unity within Christianity and among religions and people has been animated by their love for Jesus forsaken.

In this book as nowhere else, Chiara Lubich gives us a profound reconstruction of experiences, through a collection of simple letters and notes, that gives form to these two realities. These pages are presented as a kind of "narrative theology," a simple and genuine account of the discovery of a reality to be lived — a reality of love and suffering that leads to the fulfillment of Jesus' Last Testament: "that all may be one."

Chiara Lubich's treatment of unity and Jesus forsaken in their reciprocity constitutes a genuine novelty in Christian spirituality. It is a revelation, a charism, a gift to all those who are open to the mystery of unity and eager to discover, in a world such as ours, the face and the heart of Jesus forsaken present within humanity. Lubich's writings reveal God's incarnate Word communicating, through the cry of Jesus forsaken, God's own identification with humanity. This identification of God with a suffering and struggling humankind seeks to realize on earth the unity of love that is the very essence of the Trinity.

Unity and Jesus forsaken, as the pinnacles of Jesus' experience, are not simply aspects of Christian spirituality to be considered along with others, but the very foundations of the Gospel in which all the originality of Christ's message shines forth. As presented by Lubich, they embrace all the other aspects of Christian spirituality, illuminate them, and have the power to reinsert them into a new harmony that can be lived by everyone. This spirituality, lived in union with the Crucified-Risen One, transforms suffering into love in the profound experience of death and resurrection.

Chiara Lubich's book begins by speaking of unity and concludes likewise with a chapter, which I would even call prophetic, on unity. These pages present unity as God's plan for a world that is so hungry and eager for unity at all levels. However, the central chapters of the book speak of Jesus forsaken who is precisely the key to this unity, the author of unity between God and humankind, between heaven and earth, between individual men and women, peoples and nations. In this magnificent interweaving, unity is rediscovered as the divine life to be lived according to the desire and prayer of Jesus: "May they all be one. Father, may they be one in us, as you are in me and I am in you" (Jn 17:21). And Jesus crucified and forsaken is also rediscovered as the necessary passage to attain the unity that Christ himself has given us.

Unity. In air raid shelters during World War II, Chiara Lubich, with her young friends who were already following her, reread the Gospel by the light of a candle. She was deeply moved by the prayer for unity in John's Chapter 17. She understood through a supernatural intuition that it was for this that she and her companions were born, namely, to live for the ideal that all may be one. These words of John, read and lived, illumined one another and became the key to their understanding of all the other words of the Gospel.

It was a wonderful discovery. In a flash, Chiara Lubich understood that the life of God-Love, the trinitarian life, is unity ("As you are in me and I am in you."); and that this love and unity must become the life of all Christians who can actually live the very "way" of the Trinity. The experience of such a life of unity that impels us to live for one another, with one another, "making ourselves one" with our neighbor, raises our life to a continual and wonderful supernatural level, to a height where love is the supreme law, the primary and indispensable condition of all other actions. By living in God, by living God's own trinitarian life of unity, we discover how God sees and wants things to be.

There is no doubt that a supernatural wisdom, a charism, lies at the basis of such a new and lofty discovery. This actual communitarian life of unity, I might say, was practically unknown, unheard of up to that moment in the church; even though it had been sensed and preached in the history of Christian spirituality. It can be affirmed that here we are in the presence of a charism born from a page of the Gospel which in this instance is not the page of poverty, of prayer, or of the works of mercy. Rather it is the page that reveals the mystery of unity, the very purpose of Christ's coming among humankind, of his very death and resurrection.

Unity, the very life of God, the ultimate standard of life, has as its effect the desire and the obligation to be like Jesus, to be Jesus, to live like him and in him, to allow oneself to live through him in order to be able to live the divine life. It involves the fundamental decision to die to self so that Jesus may live in and through oneself. But it is also the deeply moving *communitarian* experience of a new relationship with "the other," with others, of Jesus with Jesus, in order that we may die together so that "Jesus in our midst" may be the life of all.

A profound trinitarian spiritual and theological logic is the dependable foundation of all the experiences and intuitions that Chiara Lubich has written about concerning this life of unity. Her innovations raise Christian spirituality to the level of a trinitarian spirituality, a spirituality of unity in which love, and hence the demands of love, are endowed with a trinitarian dimension: "as you are in me and I am in you." Therefore, these innovations have ushered into the church a communitarian and ecclesial spirituality of "the Mystical Body." And it was precisely in 1943, the year the Focolare was born, that Pope Pius XII published his Encyclical Letter on the Church: *Mystici Corporis*.

This communal spirituality of unity bore within itself the seeds of new forms of asceticism, of apostolate, indeed, of mysticism itself. It made new demands that could no longer be measured solely by the older individualistic standards of personal Christian perfection. Rather, these demands needed to be measured against new communal standards for the spiritual life which would now be envisioned as a communitarian holiness with a trinitarian character.

Chiara Lubich, in her writing about this discovery, has revealed to us the novel spiritual realities that God had been gradually placing in her heart and in those of her companions whom she drew together as "one." Lubich's new communitarian spirituality has been verified in its incredible fruits and vital new life. At the communal center of all this life has been the extraordinary supernatural gift of the presence of "Jesus in their midst" (cf. Mt 18:20), the presence of the Risen One where people were living as one so that all may be one.

Jesus forsaken. Chiara Lubich needed to make an additional discovery in order for unity not to be an utopia. This was Jesus crucified and forsaken, who is the author and model of this unity between God and people, and between people. This discovery, or the interior revelation of this mystery, is presented in a simple episode of life that is related in the pages of this book. When on January 24, 1944, Chiara Lubich asked: What was the greatest suffering of Jesus? a rather new and unusual answer was given. The moment when Jesus suffered most was expressed in his cry from the Cross: "My God, my God, why have you forsaken me?" (Mt 27:46; Mk 15:34). From that moment on Chiara was fascinated by that cry. She spiritually penetrated "the passion of the passion of Jesus," the very soul of the one who, by becoming sin for us, experienced separation from God and cried out his deepest spiritual suffering in which would be contained and fused all the possible sufferings of humankind.

It could only be by a special grace that Jesus' cry won Chiara Lubich's attention and love for the Crucified One. Her attention to this mystery of suffering and love brings a deeper insight into something that, although glimpsed for centuries within the church, had not until that moment been given such spiritual importance. So, it was quite natural from then on to give Jesus a new name: Jesus forsaken. This new name gathers into our spiritual awareness the greatness of the suffering and love by which we have been redeemed and reconciled with the Father and among ourselves.

Free from any exegetical and theological prejudice or concern, with the wisdom of the little ones, Chiara Lubich attained to a deep understanding of the mystery of the abandonment of Jesus on the Cross. She understood that this spiritual suffering of Jesus was at once his immense love for the Father and for humanity. It was the utmost limit of his human experience, his abysmal identification with sin and with the sins of all humankind. It was therefore necessary to embrace and love Jesus forsaken within herself and in all who suffer, discovering there the face and heart of the Forsaken One. This discovery of Jesus abandoned in every pain is possible because through his identification with all humanity, he is inherent in every human suffering.

Jesus said: "To whose who love me, I shall manifest myself" (cf. Jn 14:21). Jesus forsaken reveals himself in the concreteness and universality of every face bearing the mark of pain. He presents himself to be loved and embraced in the sufferings of humankind, in every possible situation, even perhaps in the denial of God within a large strata of modern society. Sufferings no longer cause alarm but become a motive and an invitation to love more intensely, to embrace with prayer and witness each of these faces of Jesus forsaken in order to make the presence of God felt with love.

Today, at the exegetical and theological levels, in the spiritual and pastoral areas, the wisdom of the Cross and the mystery of Jesus crucified arouse great interest. Catholic, Orthodox, and Protestant theologians are fascinated by this mystery. The relation of suffering to love in the experience of Christ and in the spiritual life also arouses the interest of persons of other religions. Chiara Lubich presents her own experience of Jesus forsaken in a novel and yet universal way that touches the experience of every man and woman.

But how is it that Jesus forsaken is the key to trinitarian unity being lived among people? How, through the genius of her sanctity did Chiara Lubich find, in this

discovery of Jesus forsaken, the true author of the unity
with God and neighbor to which she had dedicated her
life?

Throughout the pages of this book, Lubich presents
her answers to these questions from her experience of
many years that has led to profound insights into the
riches that lie hidden in this mystery. For example,
Lubich understood that Jesus in his forsakenness is the
synthesis of all virtues and the fullness of holiness in
love. In the supreme instant of his abandonment, he
lives the virtues of obedient love for the Father and
self-emptying charity for all people. United in this love
with all humankind, Jesus forsaken then commits himself into the hands of the Father. "Father, into your
hands I commit my spirit" (Lk 23:46). This is how Jesus
accomplished a wonderful passage, a splendid Pasch,
from the depths of abandonment to being welcomed
into the Father's bosom, in order to emerge as the Risen
One. And, as Lubich discovered, it is the Risen One who
shares with us the unity of his risen life.

This sharing of the resurrection life of unity was also
understood by Chiara Lubich as the gift of the Holy
Spirit that comes to us from Jesus forsaken. It was from
the heart of Christ crucified and forsaken, pierced by
the centurion's lance, but really pierced by the suffering
of his soul, that the Holy Spirit was poured out. Jesus
breathed out his Spirit (cf. Jn 19:34). The blood is the
symbol of the life Jesus gave for his friends; the water is
the sign of the Holy Spirit, the trinitarian love, which is
now being poured out from the heart of Christ. This gift
of the Spirit of Christ unites the human and the divine,

and enkindles in us this one love that can unite "many" as One Body.

In this way, Chiara Lubich's experience of Jesus forsaken reveals the trinitarian mystery of the resurrection of Christ and the life of the Holy Spirit. It is this risen life of the spirit of Christ that efficaciously accomplishes the unity that brings to fulfillment Jesus' prayer at the Last Supper that all may be one. For Chiara Lubich, Jesus forsaken is therefore a reality to be lived. Jesus forsaken is a way of saying with Paul: "For I decided to know nothing among you except Jesus Christ, and him crucified" (1 Cor. 2:2). By living this spiritual reality that brings unity through a love that is trinitarian, one also fulfills Jesus' New Commandment by loving one another as he has loved us. Further, living Jesus forsaken within us and in others leads to the joy of Easter, to the Risen One who lives in us and among us. And thus we enter into the very dynamism of the trinitarian life and into the plan of the love of the Father, the Son, and the Holy Spirit for the whole of humankind.

It is precisely on the foundation of Jesus forsaken in living for the unity of all men and women that Chiara Lubich ends the pages of her book. She, and all those who follow her, live Jesus forsaken in order to realize Jesus' Testament, his priestly prayer, the very purpose of his redemptive death. To love Jesus forsaken in the problems and difficulties of the world, where we discover his face in our own life and in the lives of others, is to contribute to a more united world. To extend this love to all by taking on the burden of their suffering is to establish them in the truth and love of God. To open our hearts to all is to share with them a love that is stronger than death, that offers to all the revelation of a God who is love.

In difficulties great or small, in personal sorrows and in social sufferings, in the wounds of humankind and in the problems of the Church, there emerges the face of Jesus forsaken and the strength to love him in order to restore unity, to heal wounds, and to solve problems. To achieve all this, Chiara Lubich does not hesitate to propose the radicalism of love: "Behold: to love. To love all men and women, so that they all know what love is and love one another as Jesus wishes, this is the fervent desire of our movement."

Unity and Jesus forsaken. Here are two words of light for the Church of our time and for all the people of our era as we approach the year 2000 when the cry of the Forsaken One is more urgent and the yearning for unity is more obvious at all levels of life. Spoken from the experience of Chiara Lubich, these are words of hope: the cry from which the radiant dawn of Easter sprang, and the prayer "That all may be one." Blended together in her spirituality for all humankind, Chiara Lubich invites us to carry out in our time the wonderful plan of unity for which Christ offered his life and his Spirit.

Jesus Castellano Cervera, OCD
The Teresanum, Rome

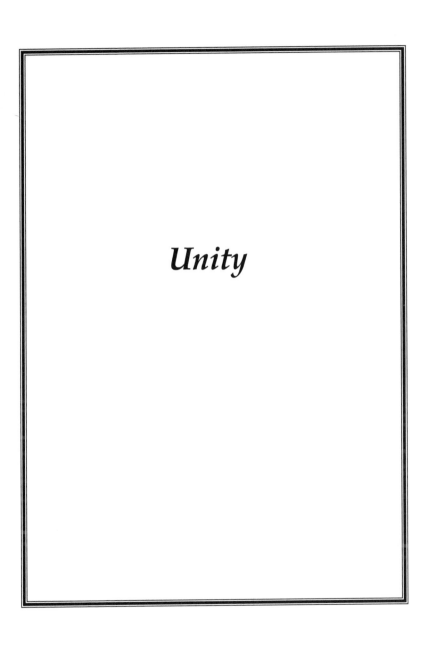

Unity

We are all aware that the modern world is strikingly full of tensions. We find them between east and west, north and south; in the Middle East and Central America; wars, threats of fresh conflicts, the explosion of terrorism and other contemporary evils. Despite all these tensions, one of the signs of the times is a trend toward unity.

One example of this, in the Christian world, comes from the Holy Spirit, stimulating the various Churches and ecclesial communities in the direction of reunion, after centuries of indifference and conflict. The popes have spoken about it: Paul VI's teachings were filled with the idea of unity. John Paul II is now a true personification of this idea, as he makes his worldwide journeys, his arms outstretched to all its peoples.

The Second Vatican Council spoke of it; its documents keep returning to this thought, which is also expressed in the establishing of new secretariats, like the one for Christian unity, for dialogue with other religions, and for dialogue with all people of good will.

Another sign is the World Council of Churches.

This tension toward unity in the world finds expression even in ideologies that we are not able to share, but which are striving to find a solution on a global scale to the great problems of today. It also expresses itself in international corporations and organizations. Unity is likewise promoted by modern means of communication, which bring the whole world to a single community or family.

Yes, this pressure toward unity certainly exists in the world, and it forms the context in which we should look at the Focolare and its spirituality.

Whenever we are asked for a definition of our spirituality, or what difference there is between the gift of God to our Movement and the gifts with which he has decorated and enriched others in the Church today and throughout the centuries, we have no hesitation in replying: unity.

Unity is our specific vocation. Unity is what characterizes the Focolare. Unity, and not other ideas or words that, in one way or another, can stand for splendid and divine ways of going to God, as for instance poverty for the Franciscan movement, obedience perhaps for the Jesuits, the little way for followers of Thérèse of Lisieux, or prayer for the Carmelites of Teresa of Avila.

The word that epitomizes our spirituality is unity. For us, unity includes every other supernatural reality, every other practice or commandment, every other religious attitude.

If unity is typical of our vocation, let's take a quick look back to the beginning of our fifty-year history, when it was first kindled like a flame, so that we can keep this flame alive in our hearts, or revive it in case it needs reviving. Let us recall certain episodes and read over again whatever we have preserved on this subject. A quick glance will help us to remain faithful disciples of the priceless gift God gave us.

Best of all, let's re-live some familiar episodes we remember from our earliest years. The war is on. A few girls and I are in a dark place somewhere — maybe a basement. We are reading the testament of Jesus by candlelight. We pursue the whole passage. Those difficult words seem to light up, one after another. We feel we understand them. But what we notice most of all is an inner conviction that they are the Magna Carta of this new life of ours and of all that is going to come into existence around us.

Some time later, conscious of the difficulty, if not impossibility, of putting such a program into practice, we feel the urge to ask Jesus for the favor of teaching us the way to live unity. Kneeling around an altar, we offer our lives to him, that — if he wishes to, and trusts us — he may use them to bring it to pass. It is — as far as we remember — the feast of Christ the King. We are struck by these words in the liturgy of the day: "Ask of me and I will give you the nations for an inheritance and the ends of the earth for your possession" (Ps 2:8). We ask, with faith.

Later on, with joy and astonishment, we will connect these events and our aspiration for unity with the encyclical which Pius XII offered to the world precisely in 1943, the year our Movement was born: the encyclical *Mystici Corporis*, on the mystical body of Christ.

One thing is clear in our soul: Unity is what God wants of us. We live only to be one with him, one with each other, and one with everybody. This marvelous vocation ties us to heaven and binds us to the one human family. What could be greater? As far as we are concerned, no ideal in life beats this.

Let's go back to our earliest days again. According to plan I give a short meditation to the group of my first companions in a room called the Massaia Hall every morning. We meet at seven o'clock. I feel the urge within not to allow my own thoughts to get in the way of the Holy Spirit; for if he thinks it worthwhile, he can enlighten me. So I prepare myself with prayer, declaring the "nothing" of me and the "all" of God. I say over and over to Jesus, in front of the Blessed Sacrament, "I am nothing, you are everything." After this prayer, I draw up a few notes. This was God's chief system for forming the girls who were my first companions in this new Ideal.[1]

Only one page remains from the notes of those years, and it dates back probably to 1946. It speaks of a single topic, the one which matters most to the nascent movement: unity.

The text is very concise — those notes generally were. After some words about the need for us to be another Jesus, God's program for us appears explicitly: "Above all else, the soul must fix its gaze on the one Father of so many children. Next, look at all created beings as children of the one Father. Let our thoughts and our hearts' affection always go beyond the bounds imposed

---

1. The word "Ideal" is used primarily to mean God, chosen as the one aim in life. Secondly, it also stands for the Focolare spirituality and the way it is lived in daily life.

by human life alone, and let's develop the habit of constantly opening ourselves up to the reality of being one human family in only one Father: God."

And it goes on:

"Jesus, our model, taught us just two things, which are one: to be children of only one Father and to be brothers and sisters to each other."

Furthermore, one virtue is emphasized which is seen to be essential to union with God and neighbor, and which is mentioned by Paul in his letters, where he urges Christians to build unity through mutual love.

"A virtue" — the note continues — "which unites the soul with God . . . is humility, emptying of self. The slightest human flaw which does not let itself be transformed by the divine, breaks the union and with grave consequences. The interior union of the soul with God presupposes the total extinction of self, humility to the most heroic degree. . . .

"Humility also leads to unity with others, since it inspires us to be as much as possible at the service of those around us.

"Every soul that wants to achieve unity must claim only one right: to serve everyone, because in everyone we serve God. . . .

"As Paul did, who was free, we want to make ourselves the slaves of all so as to win over as many as possible to Christ (cf. 1 Cor 9:19).

"Those who want to be channels for unity must maintain the deepest humility, even to the point of losing, in favor and in the service of God in their neighbor, their very selves.

"They only re-enter themselves in order to find God and pray for their brothers and sisters and for themselves.

"They constantly live as if 'emptied,' because they are totally in love with the will of God . . . and in love with their neighbor's will, whom they want to serve for the sake of God. A servant does nothing but what his master orders."

The next thought affords one a glimpse of what a great revolution this Ideal can effect:

"If all people, or at least a group, however small, were really servants of God in those around them, the world would soon belong to Christ." It says at the end of the note that love for our neighbor leads to mutual love, and therefore to unity, thus fulfilling Jesus' testament.

It goes on to state more exactly who our neighbor is: It is the brother or sister who comes our way at each moment of our day. We must love that person in a way that will induce the birth, growth, and development of Christ in him or her.

"It is important to have a clear idea of who our neighbor is.

"Our neighbor is the person who passes our way at this present moment in our life. Be ever ready to be of service to that person, because in him or her we serve God. To have a simple eye means to see only one Father, to serve God in our neighbor; to have only one neighbor: Jesus.

"The simple eye recognizes 'a Christ coming to be' in everyone. The person with a simple eye puts himself or herself at everyone's service . . . so that Christ may come and may grow in them. In each it sees a Christ being born, who as a new child of God must grow, live, do good, and must die and rise and be glorified. . . .

"We can give ourselves no peace until, through our continual service, we discover in our neighbor the spiritual face of Christ.

"In this way, we live Christ . . . and serve Christ in our neighbor so that he may grow in age and wisdom and grace. . . .

"That's why we will fulfill our Ideal (Jesus' only ideal: that all may be one) when we make the best of the moment in serving our neighbor."

So our Ideal is to bring about what Jesus prayed for on the evening of Holy Thursday. Having instituted the eucharist and the priesthood and given his disciples the New Commandment he descended (as tradition has it) an open stairway toward the torrent of Cedron: "That they may all be one" (cf. Jn 17:10, 21, 22).

All one. As long as *all* are not one, *all* those that Jesus surely had in mind, the Focolare cannot rest. That is the goal for which we were born, the purpose for which he raised us up.

No other motives or goals were present to our minds, not at that stage.

Far from our minds, for example, was the idea of ecumenism. We knew absolutely nothing about it. I remember in 1950 I was visiting a Jesuit priest named Father Boyer, the founder of *Foyer Unitas.* He asked me if our conception of unity was in function of the unity of the Church. I replied that it was not. God had not yet unveiled his plans for us in that sense.

Unity. What does it mean? In that same note from 1946 we find some explanation, expressed in terms we had learned at school: "We mustn't make a mixture, but a combination, and this will only come about if each person loses himself or herself in the heat of the flame of divine love.

"What is left if two or more [persons] 'combine'? Jesus — the One. . . .

"When unity passes through, it leaves only one trace: Christ."

In a letter of 1947 we gave a definition of unity based on our experience: "Ah! Unity, unity! What divine beauty! We have no human words to express it! It's Jesus!"

Later on, in a letter of 1948, we read again: "Unity! Who would risk speaking about it? It is as indescribable as God himself! You feel it, you see it, you enjoy it, but . . . it is indescribable! All enjoy it when it is present, all suffer when it is absent. It is peace, joy, love, ardor, the climate of heroism and the greatest generosity. It is Jesus in our midst!"

So, unity is Jesus.

Yes, unity is Jesus. When he rose, he said: "Know that I am with you always, until the end of the world" (Mt 28:20). Unity is one of the ways through which he is present in the Church, besides the eucharist, his word, his presence in those whose duty it is to evangelize or guide the community, his presence in the poor, in whom he is hidden.

We have been called to live unity at every moment of our daily lives. We sensed that this could be done by serving our neighbor. But how can we best manage to do this? Ever since the first years it has been evident to us that a good way is to "make ourselves one" with everyone we meet.

It often happens that we get caught up in our work, in a hurry, even in a wish to do God's will, and we slip into what seems to us his will. But we are really mistaken. What God wants of us more than anything else is that we make ourselves one with the person beside us, with the one who walks with us through life, with whoever we get to know day by day, even if — as can happen — it is through the media: television, radio, newspapers. Most of all he wants us to make ourselves one with people who are suffering and people deprived of God.

One of our notes from 1946 says: "We ought to be one with our neighbor, not in an idealized way, but in a real way. Not in a future way but in the present.

"Being one means feeling in ourselves what our neighbors feel. Dealing with their feelings as if they were our own, making them our own through our concern. *Being them,* doing this for the love of . . . Jesus in our neighbor.

"To be able to love our neighbors, we've got to transform this cold and stony heart of ours into a heart of flesh."

When God, in those beginning years, was teaching us how to live the way he planned for us, we spent a lot of time training ourselves in the practice of "making ourselves one" with other people.

It's no easy thing. We have to be empty of ourselves: chase our own ideas out of our heads, our own affections out of our hearts, everything out of our wills, to identify ourselves with the other person.

When I am talking to someone who would like to be part of the Focolare and would like to confide in me, although an instant reply wants to burst out, I allow a lot of time for putting aside my own ideas, until the other has poured out the full contents of his or her heart into mine. I am convinced — also because experience has taught me — that when I do this, at the end the Holy Spirit suggests exactly what I ought to say. In fact, by making myself empty I am loving, and he manifests himself if I love (cf. Jn 14:21). Thousands of times I have tested this and found that had I interrupted the speech half way through, I would have said something which was not right, something unenlightened, something merely "human." Whereas, if my love lets the speaker unburden his or her mind into mine, I am then able to give a complete answer.

If this way of loving, this way of mutual compenetration, is established between two people, then the unity which brings Christ into our midst is achieved.

If we have been called to unity, then for us the way to God passes through our neighbor. It is through this passage, which may sometimes be as dim and dark as a tunnel, that one comes to the light. This is the mysterious path God asks us to take in order to reach him.

He wants us every day and every hour to perfect this art of "making ourselves one" with other people; a tiring and exhausting one at times, but always a wonderful, vital and fruitful one too: the art of loving.

It is the cross we have got to nail ourselves to from day to day: a cross which is pre-eminently ours. For us, and for the people we love, it is our life, and if it is mutual, it is Life itself come among us. It is Jesus.

The Ideal of our life has been God from the start. He descended and is descending to live in our midst by means of unity, because "Where there is charity and love, there is God,"[2] and "Where two or three are gathered in my name, there am I in their midst" (Mt 18:20). Our way of finding God is in unity. That is the principal place where a Focolarino,[3] and whoever else chooses this road, finds him. And only if we find him there do we have the grace to find him fully in places like the eucharist, in his word, and in the hierarchy of the Church, because he gives us light on all of these supernatural realities.

Still today it is wonderful and astounding to see how from the very beginning Jesus was stimulating us to emphasize so strongly this phrase from Peter: "Above all, let your love for one another be constant" (1 Pt 4:8).

Yes, because that is the novelty of the good news: above all, mutual and continual charity. Love as the

---

2. From an ancient hymn.
3. Focolarino: A member of a men's focolare house; plural: Focolarini (also used to indicate men and women collectively). Focolarina: A member of a women's focolare house; plural: Focolarine.

foundation for the whole edifice, the soul of the whole life, the only thing which can give value to the whole.

In a letter of 1948, addressed to a group of religious who understood God's gift to the Focolare and made it their own, I wrote: "Above all (even if this 'all' included very good and sacred things, such as prayer, or the celebration of the holy Mass) be one! Then it won't any longer be you working, praying, or celebrating, but Jesus in you always."

Unity must be preserved at all costs. It costs indeed our "death" but produces this life which is Jesus. And this life, victory over and reward for our death, gives the world life through the Communion of Saints, through the witness it offers, and through the strength it gives to face the world and all its disunity, offering it a cure.

Another letter, also of 1948, says, "Let everything else go, but unity never! Where there is unity there is Jesus. . . . Don't be afraid to die. You've learned already by experience that unity requires all to die, to give life to the One. Let your death bring Life to life. This Life, which brings many other souls to life without your knowing it. Jesus said this himself: 'For *their* sakes I sanctify myself ' (Jn 17:29). To bring unity to your city and to the world, be one among yourselves. This is the only way. That unity, in which Love is alive, will give you the strength to face every type of disunity outside and to fill every void."

In another place it is written: "I would prefer to let the whole world go to pieces, so long as he is always with us. . . . Our Lord has given us an ideal . . . let us stick to it faithfully, at whatever cost, even if some day our souls might have to cry out in the torment of infinite pain: 'My God, my God, why have even you forsaken me?'. . . If we stick faithfully to our commitment (that they may be one) the world will see unity. . . . All will be one, if we will be one!

"And don't be afraid to give up everything for unity; unless we love . . . beyond all measure, unless we lose our own judgment and our own desires, we shall never be one! Wise is the one who dies so that God may live in him! And unity is the field of battle for these fighters for true life against the false life. . . . Unity above all! Arguments don't count for much, nor do the holiest of discussions, unless we give life to Jesus among us."

Just as mutual love is a commandment for Christians, so unity is the foremost of our duties. The Focolarini's Rule makes unity the norm of all norms: The first of them all is to have Jesus in our midst. This duty brings with it, however, a new joy, a joy that is full, the joy promised by Jesus with the words, "That they may possess the fullness of my joy" (Jn 17:13).

Joy, one of God's gifts to unity, is an asset to which we may not be paying sufficient attention. In our physical nature we do not usually feel health, but we notice pain. It is the same with joy in our supernatural life, which may be the reason why it does not get the notice it deserves. All the same, it is an extraordinary gift, and very highly prized.

Look at the world that surrounds us: all its apathy, all its boredom, all its sorrow, and how much thirst, how much madness for happiness. What does the phenomenon of drugs mean, the drunkenness of cinema, of television, and the rebellions in the world? Even the wars? They express a thirst for peace and justice and happiness. The human heart was made for joy. And God revealed to the first Christians, as he does to us today, the source where joy may be mined.

Because the Focolarini live on unity, they are happy. Because the Focolarini bring unity, they are dispensers of joy.

We have always said that joy is a Focolarino's uniform; and the gift that the Focolarino must give to the world is happiness.

Others are called to provide food or lodging or counsel or instruction or housing.

The gift of the Focolarini is joy, along with, or without, all those other gifts, depending on whether or not "making themselves one" with their neighbor demands that they give them food or drink, find them work, pay them a visit, bear with them, or simply share.

In any case, we are called to give comfort, to bring peace, light, and above all joy, to make the world smile.

In the first days of our life this new joy made us jubilant; we wanted to share it with everyone, and we felt grateful to God for having given it to us.

I wrote in a letter, speaking to Jesus: "The happiness that we feel in unity, which you have given us through your death, is something we want to give all the souls that touch ours. We cannot reserve it to ourselves, seeing that there are so many . . . who feel hunger and thirst for this complete peace, this boundless joy. . . . Burst our hearts . . . our very selves, in order that you alone may live in us.

. . . We have chosen you on the cross, in your most forsaken state, to be our all, and you have then given us paradise on earth. You are God, God, God."

We have to thank God for this joy, although we must not become attached to it, but turn it into a springboard from which to bring unity into the world.

"Do this [preserve unity]," I wrote in 1948, "as a sacrosanct *duty*, despite the fact that it will also bring you an immense joy.

"Jesus promised the fullness of joy to those who live unity. . . .

"Enjoy your unity, but for the Lord's sake, not for your own. . . .

"Let's make unity among ourselves the starting-point from which we run . . . to bring unity where there is none.

"And more: As Jesus preferred the cross for himself rather than Mount Tabor, so let us too prefer to stay with the person who is not in unity, so that we can suffer with him or her and then be certain that our love is pure."

Unity means making ourselves one with our neighbors.

But suppose there were no neighbors around? Suppose we had to be by ourselves at work or rest or relax or study?

We know the answer: Being completely submerged in the will of God in the present moment, the unique will of God which varies in each person's case, all together we become the will of God. And, since God and the will of God are identical, this is how we live our "being-God-by-participation": Thereby we are one with him and with each other.

I recall that from 1947 on, a method we used for having unity was precisely doing God's will to express our love for him concretely.

A letter to the first Focolarine says:

"Get just one idea fixed in your heads. It was always one idea that produced great saints. And our idea is this: unity (union with God): 'Yes, Father!'

"At each present moment, let us repeat 'Yes, Father,' to his will. Yes, yes, yes, always and only yes. This will make you share in our unity, which is found only in God.

"His will is the bond between us, and it consumes us in him and in each other. . . .

"Unity means I will what he wills. . . .

"Unity: continual direct communion with God with the radical mortification of all that is not God in the present moment. I want nothing but God. . . . Unity: among ourselves, in this stupendous communion of souls all over the world, shut in and secured behind nothing but the love of God."

So our Ideal is unity and nothing else. And this has got to be emphasized even today, in fact, today a lot more than at our beginnings. In those days, under the impulse of the Holy Spirit, it was perfectly clear. It is quite evident now to the Focolarini and the other members of the Movement. It goes without saying that we have unity in our focolare houses and likewise, I trust, in the "nucleuses" of the Volunteers, the Gen units and so on.[4] But in the Movement at large? Among all our other friends?

Is there not a danger that in certain places ours may appear to be a Movement for the living and diffusion of the Word of Life,[5] rather than a Movement for unity?

To live the Word is surely an excellent thing, but this practice too has to happen within the reality of unity. Unity has to come first.

If we believe that we can sum up our Ideal as "The choice of God," we are wrong, because that is something present in every spirituality. It is practiced by Francis, Catherine, Dominic, Ignatius and all the saints.

If we think our spirituality focuses on "The will of God," we have missed the point again. All the saints have "willed" the will of God.

---

4. The Volunteers, short for "Volunteers for God," are members of the Focolare, who are particularly committed to bringing the spirit of the gospel in their workplaces and in all structures of society. They meet regularly in small groups called nucleuses. "Gen" stands for "New Generation," the youth of the Focolare, who meet regularly in "Gen units."

5. It has been a custom in the Focolare Movement from the time it started in the early 1940s to pick out a phrase from the gospel and apply it to one's daily life for a set period of time (normally a month). This practice brings about a re-evangelization of life. The magazine *Living City* publishes a commentary, composed by Chiara Lubich, on this same Word of Life, which gets reprinted and diffused in what is, given the extensive development of the Movement, a very considerable number of copies all over the world. This practice is what the text alludes to. Cf. Chiara Lubich, *From Scripture to Life* (New York: New City Press, 1991), 7-9 and *Unity Our Adventure* (New York: New City Press, 1987), 64-65.

If we affirm that we must walk along the path of love, we have still not picked out what makes our spirituality different. Other spiritualities emphasize the same New Commandment; consequently it is an inadequate way to define our vocation.

We have to choose God in the way he wants to be chosen, love him in other words by concretely realizing his testament. We must do his will, which in our case means unity; love, by "making ourselves one" with our neighbor; love one another to the point of being consumed in one. We must embrace Jesus forsaken who is, as we shall see further on, the key to unity and has therefore always to be loved with unity in view. We must live the Word of Life, having laid first the foundation of continuous mutual love for each other, living the Word as further nourishment for that love.

At the beginning of the Focolare, to live the Word represented of course a certain novelty, but it was more the sharing of the experiences it gave us (for our evangelization and sanctification) that characterized our life.

And so the Word too must serve unity, because unity stands at the summit of the thought of Christ, synthesizing and summarizing his commandments. This is what Jesus always had us understand. What God wants most of all of us, as the Focolare Movement — which at one time was also called the Movement of Unity — is that we give rise to living cells all over the place, increasingly fervent, with Christ in their midst; more and more of them, so that we set fires far and wide in

families, offices, factories, schools, parishes, monaster-
ies, to feed a conflagration of the love of God in the
Church and in society. It is not for nothing that they
call us Focolarini[6] and our homes focolare houses. Only
by living in this way can we be certain of being on the
right track. Even though in some places or nations we
may be only a "little flock," we are still authentic,
belonging to him, and with our thrust toward the fulfillment of "That they all may be one."

This is the only adjustment or readjustment that we
need in order to be able to hope for all of God's
blessings.

After all, God's agenda for the Focolare has been this
from the outset: reach out to one's own environment,
achieving unity with each neighbor while maintaining
openness to all others.

"Your first responsibility," so says again one of the
letters already quoted, "is to see to it that all of your
confreres be one, without excluding other neighbors
whom God places near you. Die . . . completely in the
Jesus among you! Have everything in common . . . then
Jesus will draw to unity, one by one, those who live
alongside you, and will prepare for unity those afar. Just
as every object which floats by a whirlpool in the sea or
in a lake is irreparably drawn by the vortex (a whirlpool
is formed by the meeting of two currents. . . . Isn't this
too a symbol of unity?), so every person who meets Jesus
(Jesus among us) will be lost in his love irretrievably.

---

6. Literally "people of fire."

My hope is that Jesus among you will cast his nets into the wide world of your Order and that the daily catch will be miraculous."

On earth we live as part of the Church militant. We cannot wage war without weaponry or without an objective. The weapon is Christ alive in the most perfect unity between us. The objective is: "That they may all be one."

We cannot but see every person we encounter on the street as a candidate for unity. God certainly wants to see that person in the Church living in full unity with his or her brothers and sisters. This is Jesus' dream.

Jesus Forsaken:
Key to Unity
With God

The Discovery of Jesus Forsaken

*I*n the preceding pages, we have begun a study of that characteristic pivot of our spirituality which is unity, picking up the first rays of this divine idea when it appeared at the start of the Focolare. It gave us the joyful and exciting conviction that when we fulfill our specific vocation, unity being what God wants of us, the Risen One is alive among us, in the midst of the world where we are living.

As a result, from the beginning of the Focolare until now we have committed ourselves to kindling that divine presence among all who take part in our gatherings, in our various meetings, in every form of coming together, often reminding ourselves of the original counsels received from the Holy Spirit, those ideas which first occupied our thoughts for the realization of unity.

This profound experience of unity was such a gift to us, such an important centering on the special charism of the Focolare, that it triggered a communal conversion, like a sort of death and resurrection. We can certainly not make progress without continuing to do our full part to deserve the constant presence of the Risen Jesus in our midst.

We would have liked now to go straight into a complete survey of our history, to see how this idea of unity has formed the background, the framework, and the goal of our entire journey; how it has animated all

43

of our spirituality, our lifestyles, the organization of the Work of Mary,[1] its various structures, the very vows of the consecrated persons within it; how unity poses itself as the general and specific purpose of the Focolare. But as we see it, it would not be good to release ourselves from what we feel is a demand of the Holy Spirit. If since the beginning the Holy Spirit has announced unity to us as the characteristic of our spiritual path, he has also revealed, also since then, the key to its achievement.

We feel urged to pause now not only by a legitimate desire, but also by the Church's guidance. To safeguard the authenticity of their inspiration, the Church invites religious families and Movements to refashion themselves in conformity to the times when the Holy Spirit brought them to birth. When we look back to the beginnings of the Focolare, we see that, even before we had acquired ideas about the way to realize unity, a model was proposed to us, a figure, a life: that of him who was able to truly "make himself one" with all the human beings who have lived in the past, live now in the present, and will live in the future. He brought about unity, paying for it with the cross, his blood, and his cry; he who has given his presence to the Church as the Risen One for all time, until the end of the world: Jesus crucified and forsaken.

His reality, and our understanding of him, preceded, even in time, every other consideration. If we are right

---

1. The official name of the Focolare Movement, under which it is approved by the Catholic Church.

to keep 7 December 1943 (the date of my consecration to God) as the beginning of our story, we have to remember that on 24 January 1944, Jesus forsaken had already presented himself to our mind and to our heart.

But let us proceed in proper order.

As we have done for the theme of unity, so too for Jesus forsaken, to recall the first thoughts we had about him, we will try to remember episodes and circumstances and read the notes we have kept. They are familiar events and thoughts, but even today we need to pass them in review for the sake of a more complete analysis of this theme.

A first episode was the encounter with Jesus forsaken at Dori's[2] house, an encounter which this time we will let her describe herself.

She tells: "We went in search of the poor and it was probably from them that I caught an infection on my face. I was covered with sores. The medicines I took did not halt the disease. But, with my face appropriately protected, I kept on going to Mass and to our Saturday meetings.

"It was cold, and to go outside under such conditions could have been bad for me. Since my family would not let me go out, Chiara asked a Capuchin priest to bring me Communion. While I was making my thanksgiving after receiving the eucharist, the priest asked Chiara what in her opinion was the moment of Jesus' greatest suffering during his passion. She replied she had always heard that it was the pain he felt in the Garden of Gethsemani. Then the priest remarked: 'But I believe, rather, that it was

---

2. Dori Zamboni, one of the first women Focolarine in the Movement.

what he felt on the cross, when he cried out: "My God, my God, why have you forsaken me?" ' (Mt 47:26).

"As soon as the priest left, I turned to Chiara. Having overheard their conversation, I felt sure she would give me an explanation. Instead, she said: 'If Jesus' greatest pain was his abandonment by his Father, we will choose him as our Ideal and that is the way we will follow him.'

"At that moment, in my mind and imagination, I became convinced that our Ideal was the Jesus of the contorted face crying out to the Father. And my poor facial sores, which I saw as shadows of his pain, were a joy to me, because they made me resemble him a little. From that day on, Chiara spoke to me often, in fact constantly, of Jesus forsaken. He was *the* living personality in our lives."

Let's go on to a second episode, and another of our practices of those early days.

As I have said at other times, the various aspects of the new life springing up in us often arose out of a concrete step. The practice of what we called "making a stack," that is, heaping our few poor articles of clothing together, was the simple way we started living poverty and learning to use our goods properly.[3]

---

3. The author amplifies this point in another conversation: "It was no great sacrifice for us to take off our winter gloves and give them to someone who had to spend hours out in the snow begging. . . . Why not give up whatever we could do without, and give it to those who were dying of hunger and cold so as to raise their standard of living through the countless little acts of relief that Christian love might suggest?" (Chiara Lubich, *May They All Be One* [New York: New City Press, 1985], 46-47).

"Putting our books away in the attic" was the beginning of a new kind of knowledge.[4]

Eliminating from our vocabulary the word "apostolate," which was misunderstood in those days, was the starting point of spreading the love of God we discovered.

Writing a letter of invitation, out of sheer obedience, to forty-odd people we had never met — following a method we thought artificial, a model of "non-relationship" — was the premise to that broadening flood of short letters which became the initial bond between people in the nascent movement.

Again, eliminating all furniture from our little house, keeping nothing but mattresses for sleeping on the floor, was the beginning of a new style of interior decorating, simple and harmonious, and became simultaneously the first outward expression of our typical spiritual life. At that time, we hung one single object on the wall: a picture portraying Jesus forsaken, to bring home to us that he alone had to be the treasure of our existence. Each morning when we woke up, we formulated this decision in a brief prayer: "Because you are forsaken . . ." to which we added, as we turned to Mary, "Because you are desolate . . ."[5]

---

4. The author alludes to her experience of forgoing her studies so as to devote her time to the new-born community springing up around her.

5. This is a prayer to Jesus, remembering also the suffering of Mary at the foot of the cross, offering him all the events of the day to come. "Because you are forsaken Jesus, because you are desolate Mary, we offer you this day."

This stood for a unique, radical choice: Jesus forsaken.

Our letters at that time used to underline this: "Forget everything . . . even the sublimest things; let yourself be ruled by a single idea, by one God, who must penetrate every fiber of your being: Jesus crucified" (21 July 1945).

"Are you familiar with the lives of the saints? . . . Each one could be expressed in a single word: Jesus crucified; . . . Christ's wounds were their resting-place; Christ's blood was the health-giving bath of their souls; the wound in Christ's side was the casket that they filled with their love.

"Ask of Jesus crucified, in the name of his heart-rending cry, a passion for his passion. . . .

"He must be everything for you" (21 July 1945).

Jesus forsaken was the only book we wanted to read.

"Yes, true enough, I'm going to college, but there isn't any book, no matter how beautiful and profound, that gives my soul as much strength and above all as much love as Jesus crucified" (7 June 1944).

And again:

"But above all, learn from one book . . . Jesus crucified, who was abandoned by everybody. He who cries out: 'My God, my God, why have you forsaken me?' Oh! if that divine face, contorted in agony, those reddened eyes, which still look on you with kindness, forgetting my sins and yours which reduced him to this, could be always before your gaze!" (30 January 1944).

This radical choice was renewed from time to time in the years that followed.

A letter of 1948 says:

"Forget about everything in life: office, work, people, responsibilities, hunger, thirst, rest, even your own soul . . . in order to possess nobody else but him! This is everything . . . to love the way he loved us, even to the point of feeling forsaken by his Father for our sake" (14 August 1948).

And in 1949: "I have only one spouse on earth, Jesus forsaken. I have no other God but him." And so we knew nobody else but him. We had no desire to know anyone else. The Holy Spirit said to us over and over: "I know nothing but Christ, and him crucified." Love for him was exclusive; it permitted no compromises.

The choice of God, which was characteristic of the first step we took in our new way of life, became more specific: For us, to choose God meant to choose Jesus forsaken.

And here we must pause.

Reviving our ideas and remembering our first intuitions, we feel a need to give the right direction to the Focolare in whatever corner of the earth it is found. It has to be a Movement for unity and not just a Movement, for instance, for the better living of God's Word. In the same way, when we get back to our first inspirations, we are aware of the need to emphasize that our choices cannot be two: the choice of God and the further choice of Jesus forsaken. The choice for us is a single one: God in Jesus forsaken. The God of love we chose lives in him; God's will for us lives in him; in him we find the possibility to live out the New Commandment, the measure or degree of love that he is asking from us. He is *par excellence* the Word Jesus has sown in the world when he planted the seeds of the Focolare.

The actual living of Jesus forsaken gives us the possibility, the sole possibility, of having Jesus among us. It is by loving him that we shall be able to be another Mary.[6] By loving him we will work effectively for the realization of his last testament. With him we will be really living the Church. Through our love for him we will make room in our hearts, and in those of many others, for the Holy Spirit.

That is something which needs to be made clear.

It is only through love for Jesus forsaken that we will be able to avoid making mistakes, for example, in relationships forming between persons who are just starting out on this spiritual way. Mistakes could be a result of a too human interpretation of the love required by the Ideal of the God of love.

In fact, because one is at a stage when the idea is not yet very clear, due to inexperience one can think of love for God, and love for neighbor, and mutual love, and practice them in a mostly sentimental way.

---

6. *The General Statutes of the Work of Mary* (hereafter *General Statutes*) (approved by the Pontifical Council of the Laity on 29 June 1990 and again with modifications on 25 October 1994), part 1, chap. 3, art. 8 states: "[The members of the Movement] try to imitate Mary, the mother of Jesus, by committing themselves to generating and keeping alive the mystical presence of Jesus in every small or large community. . . . In her they see the one who knew best how to imitate Jesus crucified and forsaken."

As we know, even Jesus' heart felt a special love toward certain persons, but the principal way by which he manifested his love was his sacrifice on the cross and in his abandonment.

Jesus forsaken is our style of love. He teaches us to empty ourselves of everything inside us and around us, to "make ourselves one" with God; he teaches us to put aside our thoughts and attachments, to mortify our senses, to drop even our own inspirations so that we can "make ourselves one" with our neighbors, which means to serve them, to love them.

The radicalness that characterized our first choice of Jesus forsaken, the decision to see nothing else, strikes us even today as a message, a specific and urgent invitation to renew our choice of him as the only love of our life. It comes to us like a warning not only to embrace and see in all our pains a meeting with a beloved Spouse, expected and consequently welcomed "always, immediately, and joyfully,"[7] but to look at him as the gauge of our love of neighbor: a measureless measure in our duty to give our all, reserving nothing for ourselves, not even what seem to be the most spiritual values, even the most divine; to imitate his manner of loving, even to the heroic practice of all the virtues included in love.

We have to face this question: Have we truly loved *him alone* today in our heart? Or have other things taken his place, even if only for short periods of time, like our

---

7. This is a reference to a spiritual attitude adopted in the Movement, which relates to the Christian way of taking up our cross.

own ego, or other people, or activities, jobs, studies or objects, around which we have got to live in order to fulfill God's will?

Jesus forsaken was the only book we took to read. And what did the Holy Spirit lead us to read in this book?

What we saw in him was *the summit of his love, because it was the summit of his pain.* In fact, Jesus forsaken reveals *all* the love of a God.

A letter of January 1944 (one week after our first encounter with Jesus forsaken) already states:

"You will be the recipient of joys, you will be the recipient of pain and of anguish. . . . But if you only make an effort to see Jesus in the way I have presented him to you, and as I always will present him to you, in the culmination of his pain, which is the culmination of his love . . . " (30 January 1944).

And elsewhere:

". . . that's where it all is. It is the total love of God" (7 June 1944).

And again:

"Do you realize he has given us *everything*? What more could have been given us by a God who, for love, seems to have forgotten that he *is* God?" (8 December 1944).

So from the beginning, with no limit to our thankfulness, we have been aware of the superb gift in our call to follow him:

"You don't know how lucky you and we are, to be able to follow this forsaken Love.

"It is his inscrutable plan to have chosen us from among many thousands to let us hear his anguished cry: 'My God, my God, why have you forsaken me?' " (8 December 1944).

When we take these writings now and look them over, we get a feeling that this love for Jesus forsaken entered in, penetrated, and swept through our hearts like a fire which consumes everything, leaving nothing behind. A sort of divine passion, which overwhelms and transforms heart, mind, and strength. Love for Jesus forsaken was like a bolt of lightning that illuminated everything. We began to see and to understand. We were flooded with light.

Jesus forsaken shed light, for example, on the place pain occupies in the divine economy. "Jesus converted the world by his word, by his example, and by his preaching; but he transformed the world by the cross which was the way he proved his love" (1944).

What we perceived in him and his immense pain was the unfurling of his love. This vision set our hearts on fire. And it stimulated us to value our own pain as an expression of our love for him, and to become co-re-deemers in him and with him.

"Think of this . . . the Lord came to the world just once, and came as a man, and let himself be nailed to a cross. This thought gives me the strength to accept joyfully the little cross that we always carry with us" (1944).

"A person who knows what Love is and unites his own pains to those of Jesus on the cross, letting his own drop of blood fall into the sea of the divine blood of Christ, has the highest place of honor that a human being can reach: to become like God who came to earth to redeem the world" (1944).

"Believe it, a minute of your life in the white sheets of that bed is worth more, if you can accept God's gift joyfully . . . than all the work of a preacher who talks and talks with little love for the Lord" (1944).

"He has poured a great passion into my heart: a passion for himself crucified and abandoned. He who has told me from the height of his cross: 'I have allowed everything that was mine to fade away . . . everything. I am not beautiful any more; I am no longer strong; I have no peace here; up here, justice is dead; knowledge is non-existent, and truth has vanished. All I have left is my love, which wanted *to pour out for your sake* all the riches I possessed *as God.*' . . .

"As I hear those words, he seems to be calling me . . . to follow him. . . . He is the real passion of my life" (25 December 1944).

"All pain seems like nothing before him. I look forward to every pain, great or small, as God's best gift. For it is the test and proof of my own love for him" (7 June 1944).

The culmination of love was not the only thing we saw in Jesus forsaken. The place of suffering in the divine economy was not the only thing he revealed to us. In him we seemed to gaze upon the secret of sanctity.

"Remember Saint Rita. Against the dark and dim background of her little room, where her two children slept, hung the crucified God-Man. He was the secret of her love. He, and he alone.

"Shining down from that crucifix she saw the perfect example of patience, forgiveness, a tenacious, unshaken love which could hold out even till death, even to dying forsaken and abandoned.

"He was her guide along the steepest paths of sanctity, because Jesus crucified was Rita's first love" (1948).

Because he revealed all these riches, we felt he was the pearl of great price that God was offering us. His kind of love was so exalted, so extraordinary (it had reduced him to a "worm of the earth!" to "sin," for our sakes), that we were convinced no one could ever have resisted him. He is worth so very much, that there could be no fair exchange.

"We have found it! We have discovered the pearl of great price.

"Oh! Our Love!

"Oh! That man, that 'worm of the earth'! . . . He belongs to us.

"Any soul that finds him leaves everything for his embrace. She too, like the bride in the Canticle, goes in search of her treasure, loves him, and adores him!

"Which lover wouldn't be attracted by such love? I wish I could run through the whole world and collect other hearts for him! I feel that all the hearts in the world are not enough for a love as great as God" (15 June 1948).

Finally, I will conclude by sharing a very special understanding.

Our experience was still in its first year when the Spirit was already showing us Jesus forsaken as the model of a new way of life. A note in 1944 reads:

"As God he made that cry the norm of a new life, lived according to a new ideal" (8 December 1944).

So this was a new spirituality which the Spirit was pouring out upon the world. We were the first he called to this new Ideal.

In the course of time it was becoming clearer and clearer: God is calling us to unity (we have spelled out before what were the signs of this call), and Jesus forsaken is its secret; to fulfill the testament of Jesus, "that all may be one," he must come first.

In a letter of 1948, written to young men religious, we described the experience we had. We attested, ourselves somewhat surprised, to an existing connection between Jesus forsaken and unity with God and with one another.

"In my experience, only the strength of a love-pain as powerful as that of Jesus forsaken can keep a soul on its feet when it finds itself on the front lines in the cause of unity.

"This is the reason, brothers, why . . . we have taken as our goal in life, our only purpose, our everything, Jesus crucified crying out: 'My God, my God, why have you forsaken me?' This is Jesus in his deepest pain, suffering infinite disunity . . . in order to give us perfect unity, which we will reach only relatively here below, but then perfectly in heaven" (1 April 1948).

In another letter to a religious:

"Try . . . to embrace him.

"If I had not had him with me in the trials of life, this way of unity would never have opened, unless it had been Jesus' will to raise it up somewhere else in a similar way.

"Christ forsaken won every battle in me, terrible battles.

"But you have to be madly in love with him, who is the synthesis of all physical and spiritual suffering. He is medicine . . . for every kind of pain of the soul" (23 April 1948).

And so, Jesus forsaken is the key to the charism, the secret to unity. With him one will always keep moving ahead. We will need to keep this in mind for the future, against those difficult times which may come, and indeed will have to, when we may be seized with doubts whether things will progress as they did in the past. In these moments it will be good to remind ourselves of this initial light, this truly extraordinary experience.

The Fullness of Life

*W*e concluded the first meditation on Jesus forsaken with an attempt to understand all that we con-
templated in him after his initial appearance to us.

Let us now read, almost in its entirety, a letter written
30 March 1948 to a young religious. The motto of the
letter was: "My God, my God, why have even you
abandoned me?" As we will see, the most important
points about Jesus forsaken already burst forth with full
strength and clarity. This page is a small synthesis of
our doctrine about him.

Its opening words assert right away that unity is truly
understood by those who love Jesus forsaken:

"I am convinced that in its most spiritual aspect, at
its deepest and most intimate level, unity can be understood only by a person who has chosen as her portion
of life . . . Jesus forsaken, crying out 'My God, my God,
why have you forsaken me?' "

Jesus forsaken is then proclaimed as the secret and
guarantee of unity:

"Brother, now that I have found that you understand
this secret of unity, I would like to talk to you about it
forever, and I could. Try to understand that Jesus
forsaken is everything. He is the guarantee of unity.
Every light on unity we have received pours out from
that cry."

We affirm that to choose him is synonymous with giving birth to an infinite number of souls for unity:

"To choose him as our only goal, our only objective, the point of arrival for our own life is . . . to generate an infinite number of souls into unity."

The letter further states categorically that from now on this nascent spirituality will hinge on two points: unity and Jesus forsaken. It further says that these points are like two faces of the same medal:

"The book of light,[8] which the Lord is writing in my soul has two aspects. One page shines with a mysterious love: unity. Another page shines with a mysterious pain: Jesus forsaken. They are two sides to one and the same medal."

Of course, this light is new, and we have to protect it so that "holy things" are not given to people who are not ready for them.

"Brother, not everyone understands these words. Let's not give them to just anyone. Let Forsaken Love see himself surrounded only by hearts who understand him because they have felt him come into their lives, and have found in him the solution to every problem."

During that period of time, we often referred to Jesus forsaken as "the Pruned One," who seemed unwanted both by earth and heaven. We used to say: "The world

---

8. In other words, the fundamental inspiration of the Focolare: its spirituality of unity, whose key is Jesus forsaken. Cf. *General Statutes*, part 1, chap. 3, art. 8; see also, John Paul II to the priests and religious of the Focolare, on 30 April 1982, reported in the *Osservatore Romano* of 1 May 1982.

doesn't want him, not even heaven wants him; therefore we can have him all for our own."

Because he had been uprooted from both earth and heaven, he brought into unity those who were cut off, the people who had been uprooted from God. This was, indeed, the only way to unity!

In Jesus, we gain by losing; we live by dying. The grain of wheat has to die to produce the ear of grain; we need to be pruned in order to bear good fruit. That is Jesus' law, one of his paradoxes. The Holy Spirit was making us understand that in order to bring about Jesus' prayer "that all may be one" in the world, we would have to incorporate forsakenness in ourselves by welcoming Jesus forsaken in every disunity.

The following letter was written in 1949 to a few religious brothers, whose superiors had not given them permission to participate in such a novel movement:

"Is it not understood yet . . . that the greatest Ideal a human heart can yearn after — unity — is a distant dream and a mirage, if those who want it do not set their hearts exclusively upon Jesus, who was forsaken by all, even by his Father? Isn't perhaps this apparent severance [of yours] . . . from your brothers and sisters outside your college, who are fighting, living, and suffering for your own Ideal, a little piece of Jesus forsaken for you? . . .

"There is only one way that you will form yourselves to unity, and that is on the strength of embracing with all your heart Jesus forsaken, entirely wounded in body and entirely darkened in soul. . . . There lies the greatest secret and final dream of our Jesus: 'That they may all be one'! As much as we share in this infinite pain, both we and you will make an effective contribution to the unity of all brothers and sisters!" (17 February 1949).

When we read these early writings we catch on to what this God-given charism was all about: unity. And to reach that destination there was a road, a key, and a secret: Jesus forsaken.

Jesus came into the world in order that all may be one. Jesus crucified and forsaken paid for this goal. From us he wants a helping hand to reach it. The Work of Mary has made this its specific goal, and will reach it with Jesus forsaken, in him and through him.

The charism of the Focolare descended from heaven with the precise intention of the Holy Spirit to work for Jesus' cause, which the Church has always made its own: "That all may be one." Whoever those little letters were written to in the early years, they all asked one thing: dedicate yourself to unity. It is symptomatic that the first recipients were girls and men-religious, youth and adults: This meant that for an ideal which was concerned with all people, every vocation was mobilized.

Some people understood, others did not. But whoever was touched and enlightened by it felt a moral commitment to unity.

This love for Jesus forsaken entered into us like fire, and naturally stimulated us to look for him, lonely and forsaken, dwelling through grace in the depths of many human hearts:

"When you find yourself in front of a person, anyone at all, remember that in that heart lives God, God who might be abandoned by that same heart. . . . Who on earth ever remembers, in fact, that Jesus lives at the center of one's heart?" (undated).

We would find him in our neighbors, because God's abandonment was the price paid for them:

"Oh . . . give him your whole existence! Give him your will. . . . His will is all in this: Love God with your whole heart! Love your neighbor as yourself. Your neighbors . . . love them . . . and think that his or her soul is worth the immense pain of Jesus forsaken. Therefore, love them as if they *were* Jesus forsaken!" (11 January 1945).

We found him in persons left alone because of the war:

"I know that people here have been abandoned while everybody is escaping. But I do not choose to leave them. Jesus paid for them with his blood" (9 January 1945).

We found him in our young hearts' homesickness for our distant parents:

"I see him there on the cross, him too suffering homesickness and the abandonment by his Father" (25 December 1944).

We found him in tabernacles and on the cross:

"I wish I could be with you, take you by the hand, and lead you to the little church on the hill, bring you near the tabernacle, and show you two things. Down below a cold, barren tabernacle, surrounded perhaps with flowers and candles, but left alone; and inside: the living Jesus! Jesus who is God. He created you and gave you the beauties of nature and the love in your heart. . . . Full of love for this human race (and for you and me within it), this Jesus has chosen, after his death, to perpetuate his painful abandonment in this tabernacle. . . . Then I would tell you to look up at him on the cross. Has he loved you or not? Tell me. And tell me what he must have felt . . . forsaken by everybody, as he waited for death. In that painful situation not even his Father would look at him" (11 January 1945).

We found him in the midst of sorrows and misunderstandings:

"Never, never have we felt so keenly as we do today that the Lord has heard our prayers and truly loves us. We had not been aiming, of course, at the joys which flow naturally from the life of unity, but at the cross, and especially at a cry of pain issuing from the greatest pain there is: 'My God, my God, why have you forsaken me?' . . . [Our] Ideal taken for a kind of fanaticism or hysteria . . . the finger of ridicule pointed at us . . . [but] when all seems to fail, we see his divine figure in agony branded upon our hearts, a payment for the glory of the other world. Oh, heaven! Up there, unity will be perfect" (7 July 1947).

We found him in the poor we searched for, in the sick we visited, in prisoners, in people who had gone astray, in unmarried mothers.

We opened our hearts to all the works of mercy that love can invent, and which the nascent Focolare would be called to sustain through its various branches. Just one name, Jesus forsaken, has been given, is given, and will eventually be given, to everybody who has been, is, or will be blessed by this love.

In those early times, what was our attitude when faced with Jesus forsaken?

We were struck most deeply by his love, and we absolutely wanted to do something for him. Not knowing at first what to do, we sought ways of manifesting our thankful love by offering him consolation:

"Woe to me if I were to hear from you that you have become lukewarm and no longer love him who is everything for us! Isn't it true that you have not forsaken him?

"I have great hope of being able to console Love with your two hearts. It would be torture if I were to see you fallen back into the life you led before — a good life all right, but without any love for God! Tell me it is not so. Reassure me. . ." (9 January 1945).

It goes without saying that consoling him means loving him:

"Look at him on the cross, bled white, sending forth an atrocious cry. You know him well, because that cry is your life. 'My God, my God, why have you forsaken me?' and he implies: 'Will you too abandon me?' And together with me you reply: 'Never, I would rather die.'

"My little sister, never abandoning love means LOV-ING HIM, POSSESSING LOVE! . . ."

Today people might think that the verb *to console,* which occurs frequently in these letters as the stance to assume when faced with Jesus forsaken, was something borrowed from popular piety, something picked up from some traditional spirituality with a touch of the medieval about it. We could say, in fact, that Jesus, now at the right hand of the Father in heaven, has no need of our consolation.

But if we analyze these writings well, we will understand its exact meaning.

The *historical* Jesus at the moment of his abandonment seemed very alive and present to our hearts. Yet, we never thought of him except in connection with the Jesus who raised his cry of abandonment in his *mystical body*, in the humanity of our time, where he had real need of our help, our consolation:

"In such infinite pain Jesus needs our consolation. What is he missing in his anguished state? He is missing God. How can we give him God? If we are united we will have him in our midst, and the Jesus who will be born of our unity will console our crucified Love! That is why we need to make our unity grow in the amount of love and of souls! We want our king to grow to gigantic proportions among us. So we will go and try to mend every broken unity, all the more because in every broken or disconnected soul we hear the cry of our Jesus more or less loudly!" (1 April 1948).

To console Jesus forsaken. We could say that it was now time to reap what he had sown, to draw interest on what he had paid for.

Another way to love him was to share his pain:

"This has been another day spent in loving, although the 'evil birds' wanted to make it cruel and ugly. I left the bomb shelter after spending six hours down there. I wasn't cold; my heart was filled with Jesus forsaken for whose love I live, suffering those discomforts that he grants me to endure, in the hope that he may be forsaken no longer" (1 January 1945).

We wanted to love him by imitating him. His abandonment stood for the absolutely limitless quality of his love. And so we felt that if we did not take care even of seemingly insignificant things, we did not love as he loved:

"First and foremost Jesus wants my love. And I can arrive at loving him his way by contemplating him in his forsaken state: He has given himself completely to me, and I've got to do the same, giving myself totally to him. I cannot have my own will any longer; my will is his. My life will be to do his will with extreme faithfulness, even in little things; because otherwise I will have done nothing for him" (2 June 1945).

Since we chose nothing but him, we preferred him to everything else:

"There are times when the will of God means pain, abandonment, and agony. To choose it as the soul's one preference is to render indestructible our souls' unity with God and hence with our neighbor" (23 April 1948).

To console him, to share his pain, to imitate him, to prefer him: He was calling us to all that.

Let us now take a closer look at the effects of this attitude of ours. They were new effects, never perhaps experienced before, and at which we marveled.

The first effect was the distinct impression of finding ourselves on a supernatural level.

Let's read this letter from 1944:

"I am wedded to him and I have tried to turn off every other desire for his sake. . . . He and his cry at being forsaken have drawn me, Mama, and they've made me step, brokenhearted, over everything else. Yes . . . he alone could have done this. He who does not want us to make light of our [more sacred] affections, but makes us feel them in the very depth of our hearts and go beyond them" (25 December 1944).

Through this love for Jesus forsaken we experienced life, supernatural life:

"Seek nothing but him, long for nothing but him; and when he comes close to your soul, embrace him impetuously and find life in him!" (23 April 1948).

Love for Jesus forsaken was developing virtues in our soul, starting from humility:

"You know how . . . in the innermost depths of my soul I bear the love for him forsaken, and how I would love to turn his cry into my life, in the deepest humility. . . . His cry is the fountain of all humility: In the final completion of his divine mission he is led by the divine will to cry of his abandonment by the Father who was perfectly one with him" (30 October 1945).

When loved, Jesus forsaken brought the soul a gentle sweetness, rest, and fire:

"Don't [try to love him] only when there is no
alternative because we are being reminded of him by our
pain . . . but prefer him at *all* times. Don't treasure the
joy and the contentment unity brings . . . but always ask
to suffer with him. He is honey to the soul, rest, and
fire" (14 August 1948).

He was consolation, companionship, fullness, serenity, love:

"You too . . . don't forget Jesus forsaken. When
everything in your life disappears, you'll find him, faithfully faithful: He who was betrayed, in order to console
everybody else who has been betrayed; a failure, to
console every other who is a failure; a void, in order to
fill up every other void; sad, in order to cheer up every
depression; the unloved, who makes up — divinely —
for every love lost or not found. Love him in the inner
chamber of your heart, which belongs and always will
belong, entirely and only to him" (20 August 1949).

This was "heavenly love," as we used to call it. This
is what God wanted for us:

"Our love, the love which must reign in our hearts,
must always be heavenly and joyous love. This is the
way the Lord wants it. . . . Let us not offend . . . this love
by complaining or being gloomy. But at all times let us
be prepared to overcome every pain with and in joy.
This is God's will for us, and we have all the necessary
grace; we just need to know how to make use of it" (8
December 1944).

This sort of life leads to a full experience of joy, as the following writings show:

"Among all the moments of the day prefer the painful ones (especially the inner feelings of being rejected and forsaken), because in these Jesus crucified and forsaken 'marries the soul.'

"This preference, a matter of the will at first, very soon becomes *felt*, so that throwing ourselves into a sea of suffering we discover ourselves in a sea of love, of complete joy. We have confirmed through continuous experience that every pain of the soul (not of the body) [9] can be annulled, and the soul feels itself refilled with the Holy Spirit, who is joy, peace, serenity. . . . More and more I understand how in this way I can overcome the death of the soul (that is, any deprivation of love or of light, of joy or of peace). It is by means of this life which is CHRIST CRUCIFIED AND FORSAKEN" (23 April 1948).

"[You have been] tested by pain, and you know the flower of real joy, which only grows from the ground of suffering. Today and just today I have learned that pain is the condition for the birth of that unique joy which can be born in a heart following Christ" (29 June 1945).

We knew the way to love Jesus forsaken already in 1945:

"Our soul is either in joy or in pain. When the soul is not singing, something is worrying it, and this some-

---

9. Described here are experiences of the first stages of the spiritual life following the way of unity. They are also valid for later stages, except for particular moments or periods, as explained further ahead.

thing has to be given at once to God. The pains can come through external things . . . they can also be interior pains (scruples, doubts, sadness, temptations, emptiness, nostalgia). All these pains have to be given to God. The swifter the gift, the sooner love descends into our hearts. . . . If you feel something, anything at all, which doesn't leave your soul in peace, whatever it is you must give it to him. . . . If you hold on to something for yourself, even just the thought of the gift you've made, you are appropriating some riches to yourself (petty riches!) which no longer belong to you" (15 April 1945).

And we explained how in this process pain was wiped out. Nevertheless, we had to move on right away to fully living the will of God in the next moment.

As another letter reads:

"But be aware, Father, that to suffer pain of the soul is not at all essential to our vocation. There will be some, but we will have to overcome it. And we will always be capable of doing so, as long as Jesus forsaken is everything for us. . . .

"Rejoice in suffering with him. Continue to love him by doing his will. All pain passes away. Our vocation is unity, the fullness of joy" (10 May 1948).

In 1945 we added more specifically that the joy which fills the soul is somewhat like the triumphal entry of God, a sort of Easter. Later on we will see how appropriate this definition is:

"Only in extreme poverty of soul, in a soul which loses itself for love, does the Lord make his triumphal entry with fullness of joy. That is why Easter meant to us a passover into a life which is joy, which will know no sunset, as long as we live in conformity with the Ideal we have chosen.

"Would you now like to know our eternal model? Jesus crucified and forsaken. Filled up with the greatest pain known in heaven or on earth, the pain of God forsaken by God, his soul, the soul of the God-Man, does not hesitate even a moment to offer this suffering to the Father: 'Father, into your hands I commend my spirit' (Lk 23:46).

"We too must always do the same. And do you know what response Jesus will give to your offering? He will give you everything, the fullness of his joy" (15 April 1945).

And we understand how the fruit of this love for Jesus forsaken is being Jesus, living Jesus:

"I want to give you this further development of our thought, in order that the light of love may shine in you more brightly. Always take everything that is yours and give it to him. Give it to him ever more immediately. The faster you give it to him the sooner you will be him. What greater thing could I tell you? And what does life in love mean, if not to copy him? If not to live him? Here is where our sanctity is: to arrive at being him, so that we can say with Paul: 'It is no longer I who live, but Christ who lives in me' (Gal 2:20)" (22 April 1945).

Jesus forsaken attracted us like a magnet, so that right from the first months (this was still in 1944) we felt drawn to put ourselves into the depths of his forsaken heart. This we identified as our proper place: right inside his wound, which we defined as "new," because we thought of it as little known, not yet sufficiently "discovered." And once inside, we used to speak about being "beyond his wound," that is, having embraced Jesus forsaken totally, so that we found ourselves beyond pain, in love. Then we felt like we were contemplating the immense love which God has poured out over the world. It is in fact from the pain of the Crucified One, reaching its climax in that cry, that redemption comes, with sanctification and deification.

"Beyond the wound" we understood truly what love is; we were consumed by love and shared in its light: the light of Love.

This was one way to express the vocation we felt to pass through abandonment in order to find God, who is Love:

"We who pursue this most beautiful and attractive Ideal, have flung ourselves heart and soul into the new wound of his abandonment. In there we are secure, because we are living in the heart of our Love. Not only that, but from there inside we see all the immensity of God's love poured out over the world. Put yourself as well [into the wound]! . . . You will find the light of love, in other words, it will become clear to you what love is, because Jesus is the light of the world" (8 December 1944).

To sum up: supernatural life, virtue, sweetness, fire, rest, consolation, fullness, companionship, peace, serenity, love, heavenly love, the light of Love, Love, Jesus, God: Those are the extraordinary fruits of this life, of the love for Jesus forsaken when, as we embrace him, he "weds our soul," as we have said.

An already familiar writing says:

"Jesus forsaken embraced, held tightly, chosen as our one and only all, consumed with us in one, while we are consumed in one with him, having become suffering with him who is Suffering: this is everything. This is how you become (by participation) God, who is Love" (1949).

And today, after more than fifty years of the Focolare's life, these effects continue to exist, indeed they have even become daily experience.

With the deepest gratitude to God, we experience in our hearts this continual flourishing of a life ever new; in our souls we are present at the repeated dawning of new light which clears everything away: doubts, distresses, worries — putting darkness to flight. We can be invaded with joys so heavenly and be so deeply moved that there would be nothing left to do during the day but to offer God holocausts of rejoicing: We notice the Holy Spirit is not far off but within reach, our light and our guide.

People who are not involved in the Work of Mary often recognize these realities in our members.

Important people of all the Christian churches, who have to travel around the world, sometimes say that they can distinguish members of the Focolare by the fruits of the Spirit which they believe they can see on their faces; they are struck, for example, not only by the witness to mutual love among the members, but especially by their joy.

Experiencing the Life of the Risen Lord

*W*e have examined what it was we were discovering in Jesus forsaken in the early days of the Focolare; we have seen where we found him, and what our attitude had to be, and finally we have emphasized the various effects produced by love for him.

Now we ask each other: What are these effects? How are these fruits to be classified?

When we spoke of unity, of our life of communion with our brothers and sisters, we understood that unity is Jesus, the Risen Christ. In unity Jesus' presence "is felt, is seen, is enjoyed. . . . All enjoy his presence, all suffer his absence. He is peace, joy, love, warmth, a climate of heroism, of extreme generosity." And these effects, this atmosphere, is the fruit of Jesus' Spirit, which is the Holy Spirit. And the Spirit of Jesus risen in our midst makes us become Jesus, and even to others we look like a continuation of him, the Body of Christ, the Church.

In fact, anyone building unity through mutual love lives the death of Christ and his resurrection: That person "experiences" the life of the Risen One, which he or she possesses within through grace. Consequently, we live the life which cannot die. Jesus says: "Whoever is alive and believes in me will never die" (Jn 11:26).

But we have also noticed that in embracing Jesus forsaken, which any Christian can do, we experience effects equal to those of unity. In fact, identical effects.

What conclusion must we draw? Granted, a Christian is not, and never can be, an isolated individual. Yet, all the same, can we infer that if we embrace Jesus forsaken, the Risen Christ makes himself fully present in each of us individually, with the same intensity, force, power, and total commitment as when he is in our midst because of our full unity?

Let's see what the Church has to say about it. And first of all, let's try to understand whether there may be some relationship between Jesus crucified and forsaken and the gift of the Holy Spirit.

The Gospel of John says: "When Jesus took the wine, he said, 'Now it is finished.' Then he bowed his head, and delivered over his spirit" (Jn 19:30).

The theologian Lyonnet makes the following comment on this passage: "John's expression, with reference to the death of Jesus, 'he bowed his head, and delivered over his spirit' is unusual. The verb 'delivered over' [his spirit] seems to have been chosen to indicate Christ's voluntary offering of his life. . . . Using a very unusual expression to refer to Jesus' death, John meant to tell us that the effect of his death was the gift of the Spirit to the community." [10]

In the [Italian] ecumenical translation of the Bible we read: "John wished to suggest that it is by means of

10. S. Lyonnet, *Il Nuovo Testamento alla luce dell'Antico* (Brescia, 1970), 92.

his death that Jesus is able to transmit the Spirit to the world."

And Yves Congar writes: "Jesus breathes upon Mary and John, who are as it were the Church at the feet of his cross. Jesus transmits the Spirit. . . . Many Fathers interpreted it this way."[11]

Commenting on John 7:39, Jerome says: "The Spirit had not yet been given, because Jesus had not been glorified, that is, he had not been crucified."[12]

Ambrose observes that "Christ crucified, thirsting, pierced, the open rock from which water flows, fulfills what he promised in John 7:38: 'At that moment, therefore, he was thirsty, when from his side he poured forth rivers of living water sufficient to quench the thirst of all.' "[13] (Water symbolizes the Spirit.) Paul says Jesus became a curse in his death on the cross so that we might receive the promise of the Spirit (cf. Gal 3:13ff).

We read in the encyclical on the mystical body: "Through his blood the Church has been enriched with an abundant participation in his Spirit. . . .

"With the shedding of his own blood on the cross Christ merited this Spirit for us."[14] "After Christ was glorified on the cross, his spirit was communicated to the Church, poured out abundantly."[15] Clearly therefore, a relationship exists between the crucified Jesus and the Spirit: Jesus procured him for us on the cross.

---

11. Yves Congar, *Je crois en l'Espirit Saint* I (Paris, 1979), 79.
12. Quoted in H. Rahner, *L'ecclesiologia dei Padri* (Rome, 1971), 380.
13. Rahner, *L'ecclesiologia*, 388.
14. Pius XII, *Mystici Corporis*, 30.
15. Pius XII, *Mystici Corporis*, 54.

But, obviously, Jesus' cross coincides with his abandonment: If being forsaken is one of the pains of Jesus on the cross, indeed the climax of his pain, then we cannot speak of his pains and of the cross, without thinking of his abandonment. To say, then, that there is a relation between the cross of Jesus and the Holy Spirit, is also to say that there is a relation between Jesus crucified and forsaken and the Holy Spirit.

All the same, though it is not yet affirmed by others, we can perhaps think that this particular pain of Jesus, his being forsaken, has a *special* relationship with the Holy Spirit. And this for the simple reason that when we give something away we have to feel its loss. At that dreadful moment on the cross, Jesus felt his detachment from the Father. But who bonded him and still bonds him to the Father in a personal communion, if not the Holy Spirit?

A theologian has said: "In the sacred texts the coming of the Holy Spirit is set in intimate relationship with the mystery of the passage of Christ to the Father. In this mystery, in fact, we find the most perfect realization of the human love of the incarnate Word, a sign of the breath of love from which the divine Spirit proceeds." [16]

But if the climax of the love of Jesus crucified comes at his abandonment, that cry is where we can find "the most perfect realization of the human love of the incarnate Word." And so, we can also think that "the sign of the breath of love from which the Holy Spirit proceeds" is in Jesus' abandonment.

---

16. M. Bordoni, *Il tempo: valore filosofico e mistero teologico* (Rome, 1965), 141-42.

In any case, there is no reason to doubt the relationship between Jesus crucified and forsaken and the gift of the Holy Spirit.

So let's go a step further. Is the Holy Spirit given by Jesus through the cross given only to the community or to individuals too?

In the Gospel of John we read: "Jesus stood up and cried out: 'If anyone thirsts, let him come to me; let him drink, who believes in me. Scripture has it: "From within him rivers of living water shall flow." ' (Here he was referring to the Spirit, whom those that came to believe in him were to receive)" (Jn 7:37-39). "From within him" — therefore from within the individual.

We read in Basil: "The Holy Spirit is present in each person who receives him, as though conferred on him alone."[17]

Congar says: "The Holy Spirit is given to the community and is given to individuals."[18]

What they say is enough to assure us that the Crucified gives the Holy Spirit to the individual Christian too.

We know what work the Holy Spirit does in each of us.

Paul says: "[God] brought us to life with Christ when we were dead in sin. By this favor you were saved. Both with and in Christ Jesus he raised us up and gave us a place in the heavens" (Eph 2:5-6).

Congar says: "During Jesus' life on earth, the Holy Spirit had in him his temple, which contained all human

---

17. Basil the Great, *Liber de Spiritu Sancto* IX, 22.
18. Yves Congar, *Credo nello Santo* II (Brescia, 1982), 22 and 25.

beings in view of assuming them as children of God. Since the Lord's glorification, the Holy Spirit has this temple in us and in the Church. He accomplishes in us the same work of birth (cf. Jn 3:3), of life as members of the body of Christ, of the consummation of this quality in our very own body, in the glorious freedom of the sons and daughters of God (cf. Rom 8:21-23)."[19]

A theologian states: "In baptism the faithful are united to Christ, who has died and is risen. In their intimate and real union they share in the heavenly triumph on the mystical level of grace while still living in this world, and they await the manifestation of glory. Christians, awakened to a new life to be fully lived in heaven, have changed their former being for a new one, that is, for the being of Christ. This radical change has come about by clothing themselves in Christ and sharing in his lot."[20]

Hence, it is true that by embracing Jesus crucified and forsaken the Holy Spirit can fully pour out his gifts even in each one of us; it is true that the Risen One can manifest himself in each one of us.

We had already understood that through the life of grace and our mutual love we were living unity to the full, which is nothing other than the Risen One among us. Now we can affirm that through the life of grace which we each possess, and by embracing Jesus crucified

---

19. Congar, *Credo,* 77-78.
20. Elio Petretto, "Commento alla lettera agli 'Efesini,'" in *Il Nuovo Testamento* II (Milan, 1977), 654.

and forsaken, the Risen One can live with his Spirit in each of us *individually,* in such a way that his effects can be experienced.

Thus we can say with the theologian Cardinal Ratzinger: "The fount of the Spirit is Christ, the crucified. But, thanks to him, every Christian is a fount of the Spirit." [21]

We can get living proof of the presence of the Holy Spirit in the individual Christian, and therefore of his effects, from the saints.

In fact, looking more closely at the "will of God," [22] we noted how these giants in the field of religion who fulfilled this will by killing their own — embracing therefore the cross of renunciation and suffering — all experienced, as they say "an ineffable beatitude ... peace, tranquillity and a truly heavenly bliss" (Frances Cabrini), "peace and calm" (Catherine of Siena), "a continual celebration" (Vincent de Paul). They experienced the fruits of the Spirit, among which is joy.

Joy! We mentioned joy in the first chapter, speaking about unity. Now we have seen how joy is an effect of our love for Jesus forsaken, because it too is a fruit of the Spirit; joy which often manifests the other fruits, sums them up, crowns them; joy the flower of love, expression of life, of fullness, of consolation, of happi-

21. J. Ratzinger, "Lo Spirito Santo come 'communio,' " in *La riscoperta dello Spirito Santo* (Milan, 1977), 258.

22. The author alludes to a series of conversations on this theme, which she gave to members of the Focolare. These are published in *A Call to Love* (New York: New City Press, 1996).

ness, of beatitude; that joy which witnesses to light in the soul.

It has been said that joy is the uniform of the Focolarino. And that is the way it is. It must be so. It cannot but be so, because the spirituality of the Focolarino is unity, and Jesus in his prayer for unity says: "that they may share my joy completely" (Jn 17:13).

Our joy, the joy of a Christian, is the joy of Jesus: not just the serene joy of children; certainly not the exuberance of the young which is purely human; nor is it being cheerful; and it is not an earthly happiness . . . . Jesus has *his* joy, as he has *his* peace.

God wants *his* joy in the Christian, in the Focolarino.

There are times when we must be thoughtful, serious, or sorrowful with those who are in these states. However, normally we must be joyful, for joy is the open flower of love, it is the smile of love upon the world.

Every time that joy does not break into our hearts, we must ask ourselves: Are we on the right track? Are we in the will of God?

But is joy *always* possible?

The testimonies that we have quoted are from the Focolare's early times, representing our first experiences.

Now many years have gone by, and certainly we are more mature. What do we think today?

First of all, I think we must affirm that the fullness of joy which comes from embracing Jesus forsaken is the norm of our life. As we must experience in ourselves the death of Christ, sharing in his passion, so we must experience in ourselves his resurrection. And the Spirit, we saw, has led us by the hand and suggested as much as we needed to know for this to become a reality in our life.

This experience of death and resurrection, then, is made easier for us by our vocation to a community life, by our going to God together. We will never be able to estimate the help our brothers and sisters give us, even without knowing it. How much courage their faith infuses in us, how much warmth their love, how we are drawn ahead by their example! We will never know how to calculate the strength given to us by the presence of Christ in our community.

All the same, there can be particular moments, special periods in life, in which it is all but impossible to make joy penetrate our hearts, despite all our good will and the sincere embracing of Jesus forsaken. They are dark moments, full of shadow, filled with the most varied spiritual pains, caused perhaps by psychosomatic states, as is often the case. Or, more rarely, they are caused by true spiritual trials, genuine agonies, which the saints, for example, have experienced, and they are called "nights of the senses" and "nights of the spirit." These are moments in which one is called to share the suffering of Jesus forsaken in such a way as not to know how to say anything other than *fiat* or "Your will be done," with one's remaining strength. God permits these moments, as he permitted the abandonment of his Son on the cross. But in us they are for our purification and our sanctification and, at times, to associate us with the redemptive work of Jesus.

Even though these painful moments exist, generally they do not regard the everyday life of the Focolarino. Whatever their spiritual age, the Focolarini are called to live in joy, to have so much of it that they communicate it to others. They are called to show to the world the risen Christ within themselves, besides his presence among them.

Using a metaphor typical of the times in which we were living, at a certain point in our story we used to say that Jesus forsaken is like a machine: Whoever passes through it comes out Jesus. And we exhorted one another not to get stuck in the machine, in other words, not to remain in suffering, but to allow the Risen One to let his life shine through us.

This is just as true today: for the youngest who are just starting out on this road, for those who have known it for a while, and for those who are, or ought to be, its teachers.

It is sometimes noticeable, instead, that this joy is not there, or that it is not full. And this is certainly not because Jesus forsaken is visiting the soul with particular trials, but because we have perhaps ceased to make him the favorite and exclusive love of our lives.

There is no resurrection without a death. There is no joy of Jesus without love for Jesus forsaken.

There is no joy of Jesus without suffering which has been loved.

If we do not have the joy of the resurrection, it means that Jesus forsaken is no longer the Ideal of our life, of our present moment. In his place there might be our work, our ego (which wants to live when it must die), or our study, activities, things, people.

The joy that God wishes to give us is special: It is the joy of the Risen Jesus, which blossoms from suffering, bursts out from renunciation, accompanies love.

And it is a contagious joy, one which can be distinguished from others, which impresses, attracts, converts. It is not a joy that you can just switch on, not a front you can use to fool yourself or others.

To possess it, then, it is necessary to choose and re-choose him every day, and love him throughout the day in the sufferings which come, in renunciations, in the mortifications required by our life as Christians and Focolarini, in the penances which we cannot overlook.

Love Jesus forsaken so that Jesus will live in us. Jesus forsaken gave himself completely; in the spirituality which is centered on him, the Risen Jesus must shine out fully, and our joy must witness to him.

In these chapters we have spoken of and quoted from several letters. Of the documents from our early days, the ones speaking of Jesus forsaken are the most numerous.

But to whom were they written?

We wrote to our friends to draw them to the same Ideal, to our parents and relatives, one by one. Through them too, we wanted to reach a lot more people. We wrote to priests, religious, and future religious. And as fire envelops all it touches, rejecting nothing and no one but grasping at everything with its flames, so does the spiritual fire burning in these letters.

"Look at him there where he is crucified and think: Suppose it were your son? Hear him crying, 'My God, my God, why have you forsaken me?'

"It is the cry that echoes every moment in my heart. Think of him dying almost in despair and nailed up like a lamb — poor Jesus! Go on . . . tell me that you too love him and that you want to make him loved by others! Tell me that, if I should die first, you will make your own the flame of my heart.

"In the name of him, crucified for love of me and of you . . . accept the wishes I send you and make them yours: That love may make you understand how much he loved you and does love you! And stir up in your heart my passion of love" (25 December 1944).

"You too . . . hurry to love Jesus crucified and forsaken by everybody, even by his Father. . . . Have my Ideal which is him: Jesus forsaken, and do all you can to see to it that he will be forsaken no more, neither by you nor by any of those who pass your way in life.

"Look around you and see how many souls there are. Try to help them love this Love, which must save the world. Make friends with your sister's friends and tell them to love this forsaken Love and everything else will be 'added unto them.' But 'everything else' doesn't matter. What matters is only to love Love!" (undated).

God urges us, therefore, to open everyone's eyes. As all were candidates for unity, all had to know the one who had paid for it, who is its key.

Nobody should remain indifferent, but all had to be aware of how much Jesus loved us.

His cry was for everyone!

From the very beginning, in fact, our hearts felt a mission:

"You know that my Love has called me to carry out a great mission. I must, I desire to make him loved by the whole world, because it was for my sake that he was crucified and forsaken! And you . . . have pity on this Jesus, who continues to knock at your heart to get some consolation from you! You must, you can embrace my Ideal! Even if your way is a little different from mine" (1 January 1945).

We felt urged, then, to speak of him to everybody.

We felt the vocation to create around him, as we called it, a "paradise of stars."

To a girl, to whom we had given the name Eli,[23] we wrote as early as 1945:

"Cry out (which meant: live!) your name to the Eternal Father and to the heart of the Virgin! Cry it out for the whole of humanity, for every sinner of the world, for our girls. . . . Cry it out from the depths of your heart. 'But why, my God, have you forsaken me?'

"Cry it out as if you were Jesus, because the heavenly Father and the mother of Jesus and of us cannot hear that cry without coming to our aid! We have such great need of help from heaven to form on earth a 'paradise of stars' for Jesus forsaken!" (30 October 1945).

Those were certainly moments of a particular grace; the letters are there to give witness to it. But they were

---

23. Derived from the Hebrew, *Eli, Eli lema sabacthani* — "My God, my God, why have you forsaken me?" (Mt 27:46).

moments which, perhaps in other ways, we are called to relive even today, and we can do it fully if it is not we who live, but the Risen One who lives in us. Through him, we understood, we too have become sources of the Spirit. We too are another Jesus. And if this is true, his word, "I came to cast fire upon the earth . . ." (Lk 12:49) becomes ours as well. We too can and must be fire for this world.

Let us, therefore, announce Jesus forsaken to all, do our best to extend and make flourish the vineyard of Jesus forsaken, namely the Focolare, which is today's realization of the "paradise of stars" mentioned before.

We should announce Jesus forsaken, however, at the right moment.

It is true that the two faces of the coin of our Ideal have been from the beginning Jesus forsaken and unity. However, the Holy Spirit urged us to first give unity to others, while preserving Jesus forsaken to ourselves.

"I show the page of unity to everyone. For myself and for those who are in the front line of unity, our ONE ALL IS JESUS FORSAKEN. . . . To the others unity, for us the abandonment. What abandonment? That which Jesus . . . has suffered. . . . 'My God, my God, why have you forsaken me?'

"To seek him like the bride in the Song of Songs is our highest duty, we who have been cast by this infinite love into the front line" (30 March 1948).

The first witness to give to the world is unity. Whoever is touched by it will know how to grasp its secret.

Indeed, for anyone who chooses unity the encounter with Jesus forsaken happens of necessity:

"Ah, brother! If you plunge yourself into this way [of unity], you will soon experience the stigmata of the abandonment! Then the Lord will dig out of your heart an infinite void . . . which you will fill immediately with Jesus forsaken" (30 March 1948).

With these wisdom-filled suggestions the Holy Spirit really got us started on the mission which our Movement has in the Church and the world: to contribute to "that all may be one" by means of a dialogue of love with everybody, a dialogue which is possible and constructive if it is preceded by witness. Dialogue, therefore, about Someone who has already been experienced, at least a little: God, who manifests himself in unity, so that we might learn to discover the love in the incarnation, in the cross, in the abandonment; so that all of us may clothe ourselves in this love, and become identified with it; so that, more and more, we may radiate in this world the Risen Jesus.

Jesus Forsaken:
Key to Unity
with Our Neighbors

*J*esus forsaken is not only a way for and a key to our souls' unity with God. He is also the key to unity with our neighbors, to the way to love them, to the way for us to love one another.

And this is an essential topic for us of the Focolare.

It is well known that from the moment this new life came to be our choice of God-Love meant to choose the way of love. In a truly divine synthesis, the Spirit made us recognize immediately all that Jesus desired from us in this characteristic commandment of his: "I give you a new commandment: Love one another" (Jn 13:34).

Unity with other people, unity between people, is therefore a subject of extreme importance for us. It is not by chance that when we are asked what we are, we are often at a loss to find any better way of replying than by telling the little story of our beginnings: the collapse of everything during the war, the choice of God and, to live up to that choice, the practice of this commandment.

We are always returning to this demand of Jesus as to the first and fundamental inspiration; it fascinates us, attracts us, and we rediscover it as new every time we consider it more closely; living it we feel that we are in our element.

We are filled with enthusiasm when we realize that if it is a subject of such great importance to us, little children of the Church, the same was true for the Church when it began. (John says, "This, remember, is the message you heard from the beginning, we should love one another," 1 Jn 3:11.) And it is of great importance also for the Church of today.

Vatican II specifies that the law of the new people of God is the commandment of love. In love, indeed, there is not just one law of Christ, but the *whole* of his law. Scripture has always affirmed that "he who loves his neighbor has fulfilled the law" (Rom 13:8). "The whole law has found its fulfillment in this one saying: 'You shall love your neighbor as yourself' " (Gal 5:14).

Love, charity, participation in that *agape* which is God's own life ("God is agape," 1 Jn 4:8), is the highest mark of Christianity; in fact, it is the whole of our religion.

The Christian who is freed from all slavery by the Spirit living in him or her, bringing the fruits of "love, joy, peace, patient endurance, kindness, generosity, faithfulness, gentleness" (Gal 5:22-23), becomes, precisely because of this same Spirit, the slave of someone: of his or her neighbor. The Christian lives life paying a perennial debt: that of serving other people (cf. Rom 13:8).

And this love that Christ commands we have for other people, the service he commands, is not made up merely of acts, one after another. It is a state of being for Christians, a state in which we reach our perfection in the best way possible. Service of one's neighbor, in fact, is the way par excellence of Christian perfection. "Love binds the rest together and makes them perfect" (Col 3:14).

Although Vatican II gives the example of the vows of religious life as an effective way of reaching sanctity, it does not hesitate to set service of one's neighbor above them (cf. LG 42), because love for one's neighbor is in truth the specific characteristic of the Christian. Paul, moreover, puts love above all charisms (cf. 1 Cor 13).

And so, if the Church thinks this way, and if this is exactly what the Holy Spirit taught speaking directly to our hearts, we can understand how important it is to know the best way to love our brothers and sisters, the most appropriate way to achieve unity with them.

Jesus said: "This is my commandment, love one another." But he did not leave this love without a model, for he added, "as I have loved you" (Jn 15:12). And he did not leave this without any explanation when he added further: "There is no greater love than this, to lay down one's life for one's friends" (Jn 15:13).

Yes, Jesus crucified and forsaken is the way to love our neighbor. His death on the cross, forsaken, is the highest, divine, heroic lesson from Jesus about the nature of love.

This vision of Jesus crucified and forsaken is what the Holy Spirit has branded on the hearts of the members of the Focolare so that they may know the meaning of love. They conform their lives to him, as much as their weaknesses allow.

We have discussed how loving means to serve, and how there is no better way of serving than "to make ourselves one" with our neighbors.

No one has equaled Jesus forsaken in making himself one with his neighbors. For this reason, he is the model of the person who loves; he is the path and the key to unity with our neighbors.

"To make ourselves one."

But what is meant and what is required by these few short words, which are so important because they stand for the way to love?

We cannot enter the hearts of other persons to comprehend them, to understand them, to share their suffering, if our spirit is rich with a worry, a judgment, a thought . . . with anything at all. "Making ourselves one" demands spirits that are poor, persons who are poor in spirit. Only with people like this is unity possible.

And who, then, do we look to in order to learn this great art of being poor in spirit, this art which, as the gospel tells, brings with it the reign of God, the kingdom of love, love in the soul? We look to Jesus forsaken. No one is poorer than he. Having lost nearly all of his disciples and having given his mother away, he also gives his life for us and experiences the terrible sensation that his Father has abandoned him.

Looking at him we understand how everything is to be given or put aside for love of our neighbors. The things of this earth must be given away or put aside, and in a certain way — should it be necessary — also the things of heaven. Looking at him who felt forsaken by God, we must be ready even to leave God for God, as we say, when love for other people demands it, and this can happen often. Ready to leave God, for example, in prayer, to "make ourselves one" with someone in need; or giving up God in that which seems to us to be an inspiration of ours, in order to be completely empty and receive into ourselves another's suffering. Looking at him, every renunciation is possible.

And "making ourselves one" implies this renunciation, even if we are also aware of the gain it will bring. People who are loved in this way are often won over to Christ. "To the weak I became a weak person, with a view to winning the weak. I have made myself all things to all men, in order to save at least some of them" (1 Cor 9:22). Once they are won over, they love in return, and then there is unity.

The Focolare's Rule says: "The life of union among the faithful . . . demands of its members a very special love for the cross and in particular for Jesus in the mystery of his passion: the divine model for all those who want to work together for the union of all with God and with one another, *the highest point of exterior, but above all, interior detachment*."[1] And it goes on to cite the cry of Jesus: "My God, my God, why have you forsaken me?"

It is Jesus forsaken, then, who is the cause of unity.

Jesus forsaken, however, is the way to unity with our neighbors also in another way.

---

1. *General Statutes,* (Rome, 1962), part 1, chap. 1, art. 2-10. The revised Statutes (Rome, 1990), part 1, chap. 2, art. 8, read: "In their commitment to live unity they look for and choose first and foremost Jesus crucified who in the height of his passion cried out, 'My God, My God, why have you forsaken me?' They see him as the way to unity with God and one another. Love for Jesus crucified and forsaken — the divine model for those who wish to work for unity — helps those who are part of the Focolare to have an exterior and, even more important, an interior detachment, that is necessary for there to be supernatural unity."

Jesus says: "I living in them, you living in me, that their unity may be complete" (Jn 17:23). Thus it is Jesus present in every Christian, who makes them perfectly one.

But how is it possible for Jesus to fulfill in us his "I living in them"?

We have looked closely at this when speaking about Jesus forsaken as the key to the soul's unity with God. It is necessary to embrace him always, generously, and without hesitation when he presents himself in the suffering of each day, in the renunciations which the Christian life and all the virtues involve.

Then the Risen One, who we hope is already in us by grace, shines out in all his splendor; the gifts of the Spirit flow into our souls. It is an Easter that is celebrated again and again; Jesus lives in each one of us fully.

But if Jesus lives in me, and he lives also in my neighbor, it is obvious that, when I meet my neighbor, we are already one, we are perfectly one.

And what has made this possible? Love for Jesus forsaken.

Jesus forsaken is also the way of unity with our neighbor because he helps us to rebuild unity each time it has been shattered. It can happen that we have already experienced that full joy, that peace, that light, that ardor, that readiness to love, all those fruits of the Spirit which are produced by the New Commandment when it is put into practice. It may be, that is, that we already know what is implied by the presence of Jesus among two or more Christians who are united in his name. And we may have experienced what tremendous meaning it gives to our existence, even in its details: how it has shed light on circumstances, things and people. But all of a sudden an act of pride, arrogance, or a speck of selfishness on the part of one or the other, might make us plunge back into an existence similar to the life we lived before knowing Jesus more fully, an existence without warmth and color, if not worse. An uneasiness invades our soul; everything loses meaning. We do not understand why we began to live this way. The most important element is missing. He who made our life full, who had made us brim full of joy, is missing. It is as if a supernatural sun had gone down.

What can we do?

In that moment only the memory of the dark forsakenness, into which his divine soul had been plunged, can give us light. Would not all Jesus' life, which had been lived entirely for his Father, lose its value for him if, at the climax of this offering, his Father abandoned him? What sense was there in dying now? But he did not doubt: "Father, into your hands I commend my spirit!" (Lk 23:46).

Troubled as our souls are by a small or large disunity, aware of sharing a little in that agony of his, we go deep into our hearts and embrace our suffering. And then we run to our brother or sister to rebuild full harmony — whether we or they were the guilty party. (The gospel, when it asks us not to bring our gift to the altar before being reconciled with our neighbor, does not distinguish between the guilty and the innocent.) And Jesus returns among us, bringing with him strength and happiness again.

Jesus forsaken is always the key to every unity that is re-established.

Jesus in his abandonment is the path to unity with our neighbor also in another way — a mysterious but real one.

He said: "I, once I am lifted up from the earth, will draw all men to myself" (Jn 12:32); that is, I will make all one.

If it is true that Christ lives in the Christian, the Christian can, in a certain way, repeat this word about himself or herself. We do not know how much has been contributed to unity by those living crucifixes who, day by day, are raised by God's will upon the cross of brief or lasting illnesses or even deaths offered for the Focolare. Only God knows. Certainly their gift is always of tremendous worth if in the divine economy suffering is the most fruitful element.

But who do all these people look to, as they offer their Mass for the aims of the Focolare? They look to him, to whose passion they unite their own, so that all humankind "may be one."

Jesus forsaken, lastly, is the cause of unity with our neighbor also because we see him, some semblance of him, in all those who suffer. We see him in those who are troubled, in society's rejects, in the persecuted, in the needy, in those who suffer hunger and thirst, in the naked, sick, dying, in the homeless. We see him in prisoners: Who is more a prisoner and pinned down than he, in a bodily sense but also in his soul, because of the terrifying sensation that he has been abandoned by the Father with whom he is perfectly one?

We see him in those who doubt. What greater doubt than his, when for us he seems to believe the absurdest of absurdities: that God forsakes God?

We see him in the afflicted, in the disconsolate, in the forsaken, in failures, in the betrayed, in outcasts, in the victims of misfortune or of impossible situations, in the disorientated, in the defenseless, the desperate, or those drowned in fear.

We see him also in the sinner, because for us he made himself sin, a curse (cf. Gal 3:13).

In all of these persons, in all those who suffer pain of soul or body, it is not difficult to recognize his face. And because we see his face, we love him.

Thus, his image, which these suffering people remind us of, is the cause of our love. Jesus forsaken is the pathway to unity with them. And then, once loved, more often than not they love in their turn. And unity is achieved.

Hence we understand how the members of the Focolare, because they love Jesus forsaken, are open to love the whole of humanity and to direct people toward unity wherever they meet them.

Indeed, they feel so deeply the need of this love for him that it has for decades now become a practice for all of them to "consecrate themselves" to Jesus forsaken. The more committed persons in the Movement do so, like the Focolarini, the priests, the religious, the married

people, the volunteers.[2] The young people do so as well.
Even the children do so. They all understand that this
is the key of their Ideal.

Therefore they vow themselves to Jesus forsaken, as
a way of making an explicit vow to love, because he is
love.

But the Focolare loves Jesus forsaken in humanity not
only through its individual members, but also as a whole
and through its various sections. The mass movements,[3]
for example, love Jesus forsaken in the respective problems they deal with, problems which always manifest
one of his faces.

Because of him, the New Families Movement, for
instance, finds itself successfully facing the problems of
orphans: Who is more the figure of an orphan than Jesus
in that moment on the cross? Or the widows: Who is
more alone than he, without protection or company?
And likewise this holds true for the problems of separations, divorces, the aged, and the generation gap.

Because of him, the New Humanity Movement
strives to solve the thousands and thousands of problems humanity faces in all its sectors: in the world of
work — the problems of unemployment, and the tensions between social classes; in the political world — the

---

2. This refers to the various types of commitment present in the
Movement. These are explained in detail in F. Zambonini, *Chiara
Lubich—A Life for Unity* (London/New York/Manila: New City, 1992),
72-78.

3. The "mass movements" within the Focolare are those listed in the
following paragraphs. Cf. Zambonini, *Chiara Lubich,* 72-80.

problems of human rights, and of the relationship between political parties.

Because of him, it works to give a reply to the world's
problems in health and education: Who is more similar
to those in need of instruction, than Jesus, the Word of
God, who for us made himself ignorance in his "why"?

Because of him, the Priest's Movement offers a solution to the challenges of priests, of those who are lonely
or elderly, of the sometimes insufficient communion
among them, of their duty to be united to the bishops;
to the concerns for vocations, and of seminaries.

The Parish Movement seeks to respond to all the
challenges of the Church in the parish, with its liturgical
ceremonies, its many activities and associations, but
especially with its need to be a living community.

Because of him, the movements of men and women
religious can respond to the many challenges of religious
families: the renewal of their spirit, the return to the
observance of their Rules, unity between religious and
their superiors, vocations, unity between the various
religious families.

Because of him, our youth movements (the Gen and
Young People for a United World) give a hand to find
the solution to the grave problems young people and
children face today.

It is necessary to underline, however, that the Focolare does not have as its direct aim the renewal of the
family, of youth, or of the various spheres of society.
Nor does it have as its immediate goal that of solving
the problems of religious families, of priests, of semi-

narians, of parishes, even though in practice it contributes toward solving and renewing all of these.

The aim of the Focolare is to contribute toward the realization of Jesus' last will and testament in the world. And only for this end does it have its mass movements, which aim at renewing youth, families, parishes, society, priests, and religious. They strive to weave the various components of the Christian world into a single fabric, and to show to the world what the Church is like when Christ, the Risen One, is in the midst of his children.

It is above all through this witness of unity, bringing the presence of Christ and his Spirit who renews everything, that we feel the Focolare can share the present concerns and sufferings of the Church. This witness, moreover, is the basis for our every apostolic activity.

Also the various regions of the Third World, to which the Church gives so much care and attention (with its many needs and potential, but its few workers) are for us an echo of the cry of Jesus forsaken to which we attempt to respond in some way.

Likewise, the Church behind the Iron Curtain was to our hearts like our great Jesus crying out his forsakenness. With this in mind, the words of a bishop from one of those countries, when he heard us speaking of this aspect of Jesus' passion, are always present to us: "Jesus forsaken is how the Church lives its passion today."

Lastly, we come to three of the most important objectives of the Church today, for which, after the

Second Vatican Council, it has opened three great dialogues.

In the course of its more than fifty years of history, the Focolare has also come to recognize its principal aims in these same objectives: the reunion of Christians; the dialogue with other religions; the encounter with the widespread problem of atheism in the world.

Our experience tells us that the Focolare's spirituality contains extremely useful elements for dialogue with the various Churches. This has enabled us to open and to develop constructive relationships with Christians of various denominations, so that a truly ecumenical dimension of the Focolare has come about.

These elements include: *love* as the core component of Christianity and *life* ("Your way is a way of life," said Pope John Paul II), which have touched our Orthodox brothers and sisters; *the word of God,* which we stress in a very special way, and which has begun a profound dialogue and communion with the Lutherans; *unity,* which particularly interests our Anglican brothers and sisters, starting from their authorities; and Jesus words, *"Where two or more are gathered in my name, there am I in their midst,"* which has been the key word in our dialogue with members of the Reformed Churches.

Because of these various elements that we share in common with Christians of other Churches or ecclesial communities, the Focolare has seen the collapse of centuries-old prejudices, a greater understanding of truths held by the Catholic Church, and a more objective evaluation of many situations. In everyone we often find an overpowering desire for unity.

But it has been above all through Jesus forsaken that we have seen developments in this field.

In his terrible anguish because of the uncertainty, so to speak, of his unity with the Father, Jesus forsaken really appears to be like the anti-figure of him who was always so sure of that unity. His disfigured image has been what we have always seen in the Christian world, called originally to the most perfect unity, and now subdivided into hundreds of Churches.

It is for him, for his cry rising from so many traumas, divisions, and separations, that the Focolare feels mobilized to work for the restoration of unity in the Church.

The spreading of the Focolare all over the world, moreover, has brought it into frequent contact with the faithful of other religions: including Jews, Muslims, Buddhists, Maoists, Sikhs, and Hindus. And with all of them we have found a link.

While we are united to the Jews by the priceless inheritance of the Old Testament, and while Muslims due to their concept of religious life find interesting our living the faith as a community and not just as individuals, to the faithful of the religions of the Far East we are bound in a very special way by Jesus forsaken. Others, too, have roused their interest in him. We have often heard Jews affirm, having come to know this culmination of Jesus' passion, "Then, this man was truly God" (Mk 15:39).

Yet in the faithful of the religions of the Far East that typical suffering of Jesus, which brought him to a total emptying of himself, produces a very special fascination.

They already often mortify their senses and desires seeking the "energy" (as they call it) which is the ground of everything, or God, whom sometimes they love as a person. Their asceticism is admirable. It carries them so high, that when they meet genuine Christians, they are able to have a certain perception of Christian supernatural life. It is "being," in fact, which has value for them. And when someone dies to self in order "to be one" with them and consequently lets Christ live in him or herself, or when they come into contact with the Risen One in the midst of Christians who are united, they know how to distinguish that light and that peace, effects of the Spirit, which shine from those faces. They are attracted and they ask for an explanation. This leads to speaking of our religion: a dialogue which becomes evangelization.

And there is a third dialogue, a very special one, to which the Focolare feels called. It is the dialogue with those having no religious affiliation.

We believe, in fact, that it would have been meaningless for the Focolare to be called to make Jesus' greatest suffering its own, if it were not to dedicate itself, in the midst of humanity, to those most in need.

And the most needy, the most destitute, are not even those who are dying of hunger; rather they are those who, after this life, will not know the other, because they have rejected God, or because they have put material things in his place.

To dedicate ourselves to them, whom we find not only in countries which are well known for being atheistic, but who can be met in the West as in the East, in big cities as in little villages, is, it seems to us, the first and foremost call of the Focolare; a call which is so characteristically ours, so special, that it makes us think that the other dialogues, like that with other Christians, are made to serve this one.

To love, therefore; to love all humankind, so that all may know the nature of love and may love one another as Jesus desired — this is the yearning of the Focolare.

Hence, in the times of its birth, times caressed by the powerful breath of the Holy Spirit but also threatened by nuclear warfare, the Focolare has its secret: Jesus forsaken, the one who rejoined human beings to God and to one another. With its spirituality centered around him, a true "divine nuclear bomb," as our young people call it (indeed, it seems in that cry that unity itself, which is God, is shattered; for it is God who cries out: "My God, my God why have you forsaken me?"), the Focolare feels in unison with the Church of our times, and able to pursue with the Church its goal of today and forever: to fulfill Jesus last will and testament: "That they may all be one" (Jn 17:21).

Other Books by Chiara Lubich

MEDITATIONS
Pearls of Light
by Chiara Lubich **7th printing**

"Like shafts of sunlight that break through the clouds on a dreary day, these meditations touch us and turn our most mundane activities into brightly lit God-moments."

> *Liguorian*

ISBN 1-56548 -094-5, paper 5 1/8 x 8, 134 pp., $8.95

A CALL TO LOVE
Spiritual Writings, v. 1
by Chiara Lubich **2d Printing**

"Chiara Lubich has established herself as a Christian writer of considerable proportions. Given her prolific literary output it is fitting that New City Press should issue a retrospective series of Lubich's best works, titled Spiritual Writings. The first work in this series *A Call to Love* comprises three of her most popular studies of momentous Christian living: *Our Yes to God* (1980), *The Word of Life* (1974), and *The Eucharist* (1977)."

> *B.C. Catholic*

ISBN 1-56548-077-5, 5 1/8 x 8, 180 pp., $9.95

WHEN OUR LOVE IS CHARITY
Spiritual Writings, v. 2
by Chiara Lubich

"The author draws on some of the best elements of the Catholic tradition to speak a credible word for the world today. The text actually is a compilation of three independent works with the first being the book's title. The other two sections are *Jesus in Our Midst* and *When Did We See You Lord?*"

> *The Cord*

ISBN 0-911782-53-2, paper, 5 1/8 x 8, 105 pp., $8.95

MAY THEY ALL BE ONE
by Chiara Lubich **6th printing**

Chiara tells her story and that of the Focolare Movement. The perfect book for those who wish to know more about the Focolare and the spirituality of unity.

ISBN 0-911782-46-X, paper, 4 1/2 x 7, 188 pp., $5.95

FROM SCRIPTURE TO LIFE
by Chiara Lubich

"Contains commentaries that author Chiara Lubich has written on 12 different 'Words of Life' practiced by the Focolare Movement, which she founded. . . . Each section of the book includes true stories of people who applied the teaching of the Scripture passage."

Catholic News Service
ISBN 0-911782-83-4, paper, 5 1/8 x 8, 112 pp., $6.95

JOURNEY TO HEAVEN
Spiritual Thoughts to Live
by Chiara Lubich

This is the third volume of Chiara's spiritual thoughts given in monthly conference calls. It is not only inspirational but it is a practical reference guide on how to live heavenly realities in our everyday lives.

ISBN 1-56548-093-7, paper, 5 1/8 x 8, 146 pp., $8.95

THE LOVE THAT COMES FROM GOD
Reflections on the Family
by Chiara Lubich

"I see this work as truly helpful, especially strong on viewing family through the lens of faith. I will be glad to use it and recommend it."

Sr. Barbara Markey,
Director of the Omaha Family Life Office
Author of FOCCUS *Marriage Preparation*
ISBN 1-56548-030-9, 5 1/8 x 8, 96 pp., $6.95

DIARY 1964/65
by Chiara Lubich

"Add Chiara Lubich's name to the list of extraordinary Catholic women . . . In 1964 and 1965 Chiara Lubich made several trips to North and South America to encourage the Focolarini who were establishing their work in the U.S., Argentina, and Brazil. Lubich's diary records her experiences and thoughts during these journeys."

New Oxford Review
ISBN 0-911782-55-9, 5 1/8 x 8, 188 pp., $6.95

To order call 1-800-462-5980

Also available in the same series from New City Press

A LIFE FOR UNITY
An Interview with Chiara Lubich
by Franca Zambonini   *2d Printing*

"This little book's 175 pages of text are a fast and intriguing read. The insights are uplifting and Chiara's delight in a gospel that is still new and fresh after 2,000 years is contagious. She confirms that Christians are still known by their love for one another."

> *Catholic Advocate*
>
> ISBN 0-904287-45-9, 5 1/8 x 8, 181 pp., $9.95

UNITY— OUR ADVENTURE
The Focolare Movement

This publication tells the story of an adventure: that of the Focolare movement. The book intends to offer a quick panorama of the Focolare's spirituality and history. It contains 40 color and 47 black and white photos.

> ISBN 0-911782-56-7, cloth, large format, 80 pp., $14.95

UNITED IN HIS NAME
Jesus in Our Midst in the Experience
and Thought of Chiara Lubich
by Judith Povilus

"Here is the pivotal point of the spirituality that characterizes the Focolare movement: Jesus in our midst; a way of life that judges all in terms of love and unity."

> *Robert Morneau, Aux Bishop of Green Bay*
> *Author of* A Retreat with Jessica Powers
> ISBN 1-56548-003-1, 5 1/8 x 8, 160 pp., $8.95

To order call 1-800-462-5980